San Francisco Giants 2020

A Baseball Companion

Edited by R.J. Anderson, Craig Goldstein and Bret Sayre

Baseball Prospectus

Craig Brown, Steven Goldman and David Pease, Consultant Editors
Robert Au, Harry Pavlidis and Amy Pircher, Statistics Editors

Copyright © 2020 by DIY Baseball, LLC.
All rights reserved

This book or any part thereof may not be reproduced or transmitted in any form or by any means, electronic or mechanical, including photocopying, recording, or by any information storage and retrieval system, without permission in writing from the publisher.

Limit of Liability/Disclaimer of Warranty: While the publisher and the author have used their best efforts in preparing this book, they make no representations or warranties with respect to the accuracy or completeness of the contents of this book and specifically disclaim any implied warranties of merchantability or fitness for a particular purpose. No warranty may be created or extended by sales representatives or written sales materials. The advice and strategies contained herein may not be suitable for your situation. You should consult with a professional where appropriate. Neither the publisher nor the author shall be liable for any loss of profit or any other commercial damages, including but not limited to special, incidental, consequential, or other damages.

Library of Congress Cataloging-in-Publication Data:
paperback
ISBN-13: 978-1-950716-18-0

Project Credits
Cover Design: Michael Byzewski at Aesthetic Apparatus
Interior Design and Production: Jeff Pease, Dave Pease
Layout: Jeff Pease, Dave Pease

Baseball icon courtesy of Uberux, from https://www.shareicon.net/author/uberux

Ballpark diagram courtesy of Lou Spirito/THIRTY81 Project, https://thirty81project.com/

Manufactured in the United States of America
10 9 8 7 6 5 4 3 2 1

Table of Contents

Statistical Introduction v

Part 1: Team Analysis

San Francisco Giants: Where Are You Going, Where Have You Been? . . . 3
    Craig Brown, Alexis Collins and Matthew Trueblood

Performance Graphs 7

2019 Team Performance 8

2020 Team Projections 9

Team Personnel 10

Oracle Park Stats 11

Giants Team Analysis 13

Part 2: Player Analysis

Giants Player Analysis 18

Giants Prospects 111

Part 3: Featured Articles

The Baseball Is Juiced (Again) 127
    Robert Arthur

The Moral Hazard of Playing It Safe 131
    Craig Goldstein

Index of Names 137

Statistical Introduction

Sports are, fundamentally, a blend of athletic endeavor and storytelling. Baseball, like any other sport, tells its stories in so many ways: in the arc of a game from the stands or a season from the box scores, in photos, or even in numbers. At Baseball Prospectus, we understand that statistics don't replace observation or any of baseball's stories, but complement everything else that makes the game so much fun.

What stats help us with is with patterns and precision, variance and value. This book can help you learn things you may not see from watching a game or hundred, whether it's the path of a career over time or the breadth of the entire MLB. We'd also never ask you to choose between our numbers and the experience of viewing a game from the cheap seats or the comfort of your home; our publication combines running the numbers with observations and wisdom from some of the brightest minds we can find. But if you *do* want to learn more about the numbers beyond what's on the backs of player jerseys, let us help explain.

Offense

We've revised our methodology for determining batting value. Long-time readers of the book will notice that we've retired True Average in favor of a new metric: Deserved Runs Created Plus (DRC+). Developed by Jonathan Judge and our stats team, this statistic measures everything a player does at the plate–reaching base, hitting for power, making outs, and moving runners over–and puts it on a scale where 100 equals league-average performance. A DRC+ of 150 is terrific, a DRC+ of 100 is average and a DRC+ of 75 means you better be an excellent defender.

DRC+ also does a better job than any of our previous metrics in taking contextual factors into account. The model adjusts for how the park affects performance, but also for things like the talent of the opposing pitcher, value of different types of batted-ball events, league, temperature and other factors. It's able to describe a player's expected offensive contribution than any other statistic we've found over the years, and also does a better job of predicting future performance as well.

There's a lot more to DRC+'s story, and you can read all about it in greater depth near the end of this book.

The other aspect of run-scoring is baserunning, which we quantify using Baserunning Runs. BRR not only records the value of stolen bases (or getting caught in the act), but also accounts for all the stuff that doesn't show up on the back of a baseball card: a runner's ability to go first to third on a single, or advance on a fly ball.

Defense

Where offensive value is *relatively* easy to identify and understand, defensive value is…not. Over the past dozen years, the sabermetric community has focused mostly on stats based on zone data: a real-live human person records the type of batted ball and estimated landing location, and models are created that give expected outs. From there, you can compare fielders' actual outs to those expected ones. Simple, right?

Unfortunately, zone data has two major issues. First, zone data is recorded by commercial data providers who keep the raw data private unless you pay for it. (All the statistics we build in this book and on our website use public data as inputs.) That hurts our ability to test assumptions or duplicate results. Second, over the years it has become apparent that there's quite a bit of "noise" in zone-based fielding analysis. Sometimes the conclusions drawn from zone data don't hold up to scrutiny, and sometimes the different data provided by different providers don't look anything alike, giving wildly different results. Sometimes the hard-working professional stringers or scorers might unknowingly inflict unconscious bias into the mix: for example good fielders will often be credited with more expected outs despite the data, and ballparks with high press boxes tend to score more line drives than ones with a lower press box.

Enter our Fielding Runs Above Average (FRAA). For most positions, FRAA is built from play-by-play data, which allows us to avoid the subjectivity found in many other fielding metrics. The idea is this: count how many fielding plays are made by a given player and compare that to expected plays for an average fielder at their position (based on pitcher ground ball tendencies and batter handedness). Then we adjust for park and base-out situations.

When it comes to catchers, our methodology is a little different thanks to the laundry list of responsibilities they're tasked with beyond just, well, catching and throwing the ball. By now you've probably heard about "framing" or the art of making umpires more likely to call balls outside the strike zone for strikes. To put this into one tidy number, we incorporate pitch tracking data (for the years it exists) and adjust for important factors like pitcher, umpire, batter and home-field advantage using a mixed-model approach. This grants us a number for how many strikes the catcher is personally adding to (or subtracting from) his pitchers' performance…which we then convert to runs added or lost using linear weights.

Framing is one of the biggest parts of determining catcher value, but we also take into account blocking balls from going past, whether a scorer deems it a passed ball or a wild pitch. We use a similar approach—one that really benefits from the pitch tracking data that tells us what ends up in the dirt and what doesn't. We also include a catcher's ability to prevent stolen bases and how well they field balls in play, and *finally* we come up with our FRAA for catchers.

Pitching

Both pitching and fielding make up the half of baseball that isn't run scoring: run prevention. Separating pitching from fielding is a tough task, and most recent pitching analysis has branched off from Voros McCracken's famous (and controversial) statement, "There is little if any difference among major-league pitchers in their ability to prevent hits on balls hit in the field of play." The research of the analytic community has validated this to some extent, and there are a host of "defense-independent" pitching measures that have been developed to try and extract the effect of the defense behind a hurler from the pitcher's work.

Our solution to this quandary is Deserved Run Average (DRA), our core pitching metric. DRA looks like earned run average (ERA), the tried-and-true pitching stat you've seen on every baseball broadcast or box score from the past century, but it's very different. To start, DRA takes an event-by-event look at what the pitchers does, and adjusts the value of that event based on different environmental factors like park, batter, catcher, umpire, base-out situation, run differential, inning, defense, home field advantage, pitcher role and temperature. That mixed model gives us a pitcher's expected contribution, similar to what we do for our DRC+ model for hitters and FRAA model for catchers. (Oh, and we also consider the pitcher's effect on basestealing and on balls getting past the catcher.)

It's important to note that DRA is set to the scale of runs allowed per nine innings (RA9) instead of ERA, which makes DRA's scale slightly higher than ERA's. The reason for this is because ERA tends to overrate three types of pitchers:

1. Pitchers who play in parks where scorers hand out more errors. Official scorers differ significantly in the frequency at which they assign errors to fielders.
2. Ground-ball pitchers, because a substantial proportion of errors occur on groundballs.
3. Pitchers who aren't very good. Better pitchers often allow fewer unearned runs than bad pitchers, because good pitchers tend to find ways to get out of jams.

Since the last time you picked up an edition of this book, we've also made a few minor changes to DRA to make it better. Recent research into "tunneling"—the act of throwing consecutive pitches that appear similar from a batter's point of view until after the swing decision point–data has given us a new contextual factor to account for in DRA: plate distance. This refers to the distance between successive pitches as they approach the plate, and while it has a smaller effect than factors like velocity or whiff rate, it still can help explain pitcher strikeout rate in our model.

New Pitching Metrics for 2020

We're including a few "new" pitching metrics in the book for the 2020 edition, though unlike last year, these numbers may be a little bit more familiar to those of you who have spent some time investigating baseball statistics.

Fastball Percentage

Our fastball percentage (FB%) statistic measures how frequently a pitcher throws a pitch classified as a "fastball," measured as a percentage of overall pitches thrown. We qualify three types of fastballs:

1. The traditional four-seam fastball;
2. The two-seam fastball or sinker;
3. "Hard cutters," which are pitches that have the movement profile of a cut fastball and are used as the pitcher's primary offering or in place of a more traditional fastball.

For example, a pitcher with a FB% of 67 throws any combination of these three pitches about two-thirds of the time.

Whiff Rate

Everybody loves a swing and a miss, and whiff rate (WHF) measures how frequently pitchers induce a swinging strike. To calculate WHF, we add up all the pitches thrown that ended with a swinging strike, then divide that number by a pitcher's total pitches thrown. Most often, high whiff rates correlate with high strikeout rates (and overall effective pitcher performance).

Called Strike Probability

Called Strike Probability (CSP) is a number that represents the likelihood that all of a pitcher's pitches will be called a strike while controlling for location, pitcher and batter handedness, umpire and count. Here's how it works: on each pitch, our model determines how many times (out of 100) that a similar pitch was called for a strike given those factors mentioned above, and when normalized for each batter's strike zone. Then we average the CSP for all pitches thrown by a pitcher in a season, and that gives us the yearly CSP percentage you see in the stats boxes.

As you might imagine, pitchers with a higher CSP are more likely to work in the zone, where pitchers with a lower CSP are likely locating their pitches outside the normal strike zone, for better or for worse.

Projections

Many of you aren't turning to this book just for a look at what a player has done, but for a look at what a player is going to do: the PECOTA projections. PECOTA, initially developed by Nate Silver (who has moved on to greater fame as a political analyst), consists of three parts:

1. Major-league equivalencies, which use minor-league statistics to project how a player will perform in the major leagues;
2. Baseline forecasts, which use weighted averages and regression to the mean to estimate a player's current true talent level; and
3. Aging curves, which uses the career paths of comparable players to estimate how a player's statistics are likely to change over time.

With all those important things covered, let's take a look at what's in the book this year.

Team Prospectus

Most of this book is composed of team chapters, with one for each of the 30 major-league franchises. On the first page of each chapter, you'll see a box that contains some of the key statistics for each team as well as a very inviting stadium diagram. (You can see an example of this for the Milwaukee Brewers on this very page!)

We start with the team name, their unadjusted 2019 win-loss record, and their divisional ranking. Beneath that are a host of other team statistics. **Pythag** presents an adjusted 2019 winning percentage, calculated by taking runs scored per game (**RS/G**) and runs allowed per game (**RA/G**) for the team, and running them through a version of Bill James' Pythagorean formula that was refined and improved by David Smyth and Brandon Heipp. (The formula is called "Pythagenpat," which is equally fun to type and to say.)

Next up is **DRC+**, described earlier, to indicate the overall hitting ability of the team either above or below league-average. Run prevention on the pitching side is covered by **DRA** (also mentioned earlier) and another metric: Fielding Independent Pitching (**FIP**), which calculates another ERA-like statistic based on strikeouts, walks, and home runs recorded. Defensive Efficiency Rating (**DER**) tells us the percentage of balls in play turned into outs for the team, and is a quick fielding shorthand that rounds out run prevention.

After that, we have several measures related to roster composition, as opposed to on-field performance. **B-Age** and **P-Age** tell us the average age of a team's batters and pitchers, respectively. **Salary** is the combined team payroll for all on-field players, and Doug Pappas' Marginal Dollars per Marginal Win (**M$/MW**) tells us how much money a team spent to earn production above replacement level.

Ending this batch of statistics is the number of disabled list days a team had over the season (**IL Days**) and the amount of salary paid to players on the disabled list (**$ on IL**); this final number is expressed as a percentage of total payroll.

Next to each of these stats, we've listed each team's MLB rank in that category from first to 30th. In this, first always indicates a positive outcome and 30th a negative outcome, except in the case of salary—first is highest.

After the franchise statistics, we share a few items about the team's home ballpark. There's the aforementioned diagram of the park's dimensions (including distances to the outfield wall), a graphic showing the height of the wall from the left-field pole to the right-field pole, and a table showing three-year park factors for the stadium. The park factors are displayed as indexes where 100 is average, 110 means that the park inflates the statistic in question by 10 percent, and 90 means that the park deflates the statistic in question by 10 percent.

On the second page of each team chapter, you'll find three graphs. The first is the **2019 Hit List Ranking**. This shows our Hit List Rank for the team on each day of the 2019 season and is intended to give you a picture of the ups and downs of the team's season. Hit List Rank measures overall team performance and drives the Hit List Power Rankings at the baseballprospectus.com website.

The second graph is **Committed Payroll** and helps you see how the team's payroll has compared to the MLB and divisional average payrolls over time. Payroll figures are current as of January 1, 2020; with so many free agents still unsigned as of this writing, the final 2020 figure will likely be significantly different for many teams. (In the meantime, you can always find the most current data at Baseball Prospectus' Cot's Baseball Contracts page.)

The third graph is **Farm System Ranking** and displays how the Baseball Prospectus prospect team has ranked the organization's farm system since 2007.

After the graphs, we have a **Personnel** section that lists many of the important decision-makers and upper-level field and operations staff members for the franchise, as well as any former Baseball Prospectus staff members who are currently part of the organization. (In very rare circumstances, someone might be on both lists!)

www.baseballprospectus.com

Juan Soto LF
Born: 10/25/98   Age: 21   Bats: L   Throws: L
Height: 6'1"   Weight: 185   Origin: International Free Agent, 2015

YEAR	TEAM	LVL	AGE	PA	R	2B	3B	HR	RBI	BB	K	SB	CS	AVG/OBP/SLG
2017	NAT	RK	18	27	3	1	1	0	4	2	1	0	0	.320/.370/.440
2017	HAG	A	18	96	15	5	0	3	14	10	8	1	2	.360/.427/.523
2018	HAG	A	19	74	12	5	3	5	24	14	13	2	0	.373/.486/.814
2018	POT	A+	19	73	17	3	1	7	18	11	8	0	1	.371/.466/.790
2018	HAR	AA	19	35	4	2	0	2	10	4	7	1	0	.323/.400/.581
2018	WAS	MLB	19	494	77	25	1	22	70	79	99	5	2	.292/.406/.517
2019	WAS	MLB	20	659	110	32	5	34	110	108	132	12	1	.282/.401/.548
2020	WAS	MLB	21	630	92	30	3	35	102	85	123	5	2	.284/.382/.543

Comparables: Ronald Acuña Jr., Mike Trout, Tony Conigliaro

YEAR	TEAM	LVL	AGE	PA	DRC+	VORP	BABIP	BRR	FRAA	WARP
2017	NAT	RK	18	27	135	1.5	.333	0.0	RF(9): -1.1	0.0
2017	HAG	A	18	96	181	8.0	.373	1.0	RF(19): -1.9, LF(2): -0.3	0.9
2018	HAG	A	19	74	222	14.5	.405	0.3	RF(14): 1.1, CF(2): 0.2	1.2
2018	POT	A+	19	73	260	15.4	.340	1.4	RF(14): 1.0, LF(1): 0.0	1.6
2018	HAR	AA	19	35	113	3.6	.364	0.0	LF(4): 0.6, RF(4): -0.5	0.1
2018	WAS	MLB	19	494	125	40.5	.338	-0.5	LF(114): 2.7	3.0
2019	WAS	MLB	20	659	136	49.0	.312	1.4	LF(150): -0.8	4.9
2020	WAS	MLB	21	630	133	43.6	.310	-0.1	LF 3	4.8

Position Players

After all that information and a thoughtful bylined essay covering each team, we present our player comments. These are also bylined, but due to frequent franchise shifts during the offseason, our bylines are more a rough guide than a perfect accounting of who wrote what.

Each player is listed with the major-league team that employed him as of early January 2020. If a player changed teams after that point via free agency, trade, or any other method, you'll be able to find them in the chapter for their previous squad.

As an example, take a look at the player comment for Nationals outfielder Juan Soto: the stat block that accompanies his written comment is at the top of this page. First we cover biographical information (age is as of June 30, 2020) before moving onto the stats themselves. Our statistic columns include standard identifying information like **YEAR**, **TEAM**, **LVL** (level of affiliated play) and **AGE** before getting into the numbers. Next, we provide raw, untranslated numbers like you might find on the back of your dad's baseball cards: **PA** (plate appearances), **R** (runs), **2B** (doubles), **3B** (triples), **HR** (home runs), **RBI** (runs batted in), **BB** (walks), **K** (strikeouts), **SB** (stolen bases) and **CS** (caught stealing).

Statistical Introduction - xi

Next, we have unadjusted "slash" statistics: **AVG** (batting average), **OBP** (on-base percentage) and **SLG** (slugging percentage). Following the slash line is **DRC+** (Deserved Runs Created Plus), which we described earlier as total offensive expected contribution compared to the league average.

One of our oldest active metrics, **VORP** (Value Over Replacement Player), considers offensive production, position and plate appearances. In essence, it is the number of runs contributed beyond what a replacement-level player at the same position would contribute if given the same percentage of team plate appearances. VORP does not consider the quality of a player's defense.

BABIP (batting average on balls in play) tells us how often a ball in play fell for a hit, and can help us identify whether a batter may have been lucky or not...but note that high BABIPs also tend to follow the great hitters of our time, as well as speedy singles hitters who put the ball on the ground.

The next item is **BRR** (Baserunning Runs), which covers all of a player's baserunning accomplishments including (but not limited to) swiped bags and failed attempts. Next is **FRAA** (Fielding Runs Above Average), which also includes the number of games previously played at each position noted in parentheses. Multi-position players have only their two most frequent positions listed here, but their total FRAA number reflects all positions played.

Our last column here is **WARP** (Wins Above Replacement Player). WARP estimates the total value of a player, which means for hitters it takes into account hitting runs above average (calculated using the DRC+ model), BRR and FRAA. Then, it makes an adjustment for positions played and gives the player a credit for plate appearances based upon the difference between "replacement level"—which is derived from the quality of players added to a team's roster after the start of the season–and the league average.

The final line just below the stats box is **PECOTA** data, which is discussed further in a following section.

Catchers

Catchers are a special breed, and thus they have earned their own separate box which displays some of the defensive metrics that we've built just for them. As an example, let's check out J.T. Realmuto.

The **YEAR** and **TEAM** columns match what you'd find in the other stat box. **P. COUNT** indicates the number of pitches thrown while the catcher was behind the plate, including swinging strikes, fouls and balls in play. **FRM RUNS** is the total run value the catcher provided (or cost) his team by influencing the umpire to call strikes where other catchers did not. **BLK RUNS** expresses the total run value above or below average for the catcher's ability to prevent wild pitches and passed balls. **THRW RUNS** is calculated using a similar model as the previous two statistics, and it measures a catcher's ability to throw out basestealers but also to dissuade them from testing his arm in the first place. It takes into account factors like the pitcher (including his delivery and pickoff move) and baserunner (who could be as fast as Billy Hamilton or as slow as Yonder Alonso). **TOT RUNS** is the sum of all of the previous three statistics.

Justin Verlander   RHP
Born: 02/20/83   Age: 37   Bats: R   Throws: R
Height: 6'5"   Weight: 225   Origin: Round 1, 2004 Draft (#2 overall)

YEAR	TEAM	LVL	AGE	W	L	SV	G	GS	IP	H	HR	BB/9	K/9	K	GB%	BABIP
2017	DET	MLB	34	10	8	0	28	28	172	153	23	3.5	9.2	176	34%	.283
2017	HOU	MLB	34	5	0	0	5	5	34	17	4	1.3	11.4	43	32%	.194
2018	HOU	MLB	35	16	9	0	34	34	214	156	28	1.6	12.2	290	31%	.272
2019	HOU	MLB	36	21	6	0	34	34	223	137	36	1.7	12.1	300	36%	.219
2020	HOU	MLB	37	15	6	0	29	29	184	138	28	2.3	12.1	248	35%	.274

Comparables: Zack Greinke, A.J. Burnett, Aníbal Sánchez

YEAR	TEAM	LVL	AGE	WHIP	ERA	DRA	WARP	MPH	FB%	WHF	CSP
2017	DET	MLB	34	1.28	3.82	4.03	3.0	97.7	58	11	47.8
2017	HOU	MLB	34	0.65	1.06	3.08	0.9	97.5	59.6	15.1	49.9
2018	HOU	MLB	35	0.90	2.52	2.33	7.3	97.5	61.2	16.2	51.6
2019	HOU	MLB	36	0.80	2.58	2.51	7.9	96.8	49.9	17.5	48.3
2020	HOU	MLB	37	1.01	2.75	2.95	5.3	95.8	54.6	15.1	48.2

Pitchers

Let's give our pitchers a turn, using 2019 AL Cy Young winner Justin Verlander as our example. Take a look at his stat block: the first line and the **YEAR**, **TEAM**, **LVL** and **AGE** columns are the same as in the position player example earlier.

Here too, we have a series of columns that display raw, unadjusted statistics compiled by the pitcher over the course of a season: **W** (wins), **L** (losses), **SV** (saves), **G** (games pitched), **GS** (games started), **IP** (innings pitched), **H** (hits allowed) and **HR** (home runs allowed). Next we have two statistics that are rates: **BB/9** (walks per nine innings) and **K/9** (strikeouts per nine innings), before returning to the unadjusted K (strikeouts).

Next up is **GB%** (ground ball percentage), which is the percentage of all batted balls that were hit on the ground, including both outs and hits. Remember, this is based on observational data and subject to human error, so please approach this with a healthy dose of skepticism.

BABIP (batting average on balls in play) is calculated using the same methodology as it is for position players, but it often tells us more about a pitcher than it does a hitter. With pitchers, a high BABIP is often due to poor defense or bad luck, and can often be an indicator of potential rebound, and a low BABIP may be cause to expect performance regression. (A typical league-average BABIP is close to .290-.300.)

The metrics **WHIP** (walks plus hits per inning pitched) and **ERA** (earned run average) are old standbys: WHIP measures walks and hits allowed on a per-inning basis, while ERA measures earned runs on a nine-inning basis. Neither of these stats are translated or adjusted.

DRA (Deserved Run Average) was described at length earlier, and measures how many runs the pitcher "deserved" to allow per nine innings. Please note that since we lack all the data points that would make for a "real" DRA for minor-league events, the DRA displayed for minor league partial-seasons is based off of different data. (That data is a modified version of our cFIP metric, which you can find more information about on our website.)

Just like with hitters, **WARP** (Wins Above Replacement Player) is a total value metric that puts pitchers of all stripes on the same scale as position players. We use DRA as the primary input for our calculation of WARP. You might notice that relief pitchers (due to their limited innings) may have a lower WARP than you were expecting or than you might see in other WARP-like metrics. WARP does not take leverage into account, just the actions a pitcher performs and the expected value of those actions...which ends up judging high-leverage relief pitchers differently than you might imagine given their prestige and market value.

MPH gives you the pitcher's 95th percentile velocity for the noted season, in order to give you an idea of what the *peak* fastball velocity a pitcher possesses. Since this comes from our pitch-tracking data, it is not publicly available for minor-league pitchers.

Finally, we display the three new pitching metrics we described earlier. **FB%** (fastball percentage) gives you the percentage of fastballs thrown out of all pitches. **WHF** (whiff rate) tells you the percentage of swinging strikes induced out of all pitches. **CSP** (called strike probability) expresses the likelihood of all pitches thrown to result in a called strike, after controlling for factors like handedness, umpire, pitch type, count and location.

PECOTA

All players have PECOTA projections for 2020, as well as a set of other numbers that describe the performance of comparable players according to PECOTA. All projections for 2020 are for the player at the date we went to press in early January and are projected into the league and park context as indicated by the team abbreviation. (Note that players at very low levels of the minors are too unpredictable to assess using these numbers.) All PECOTA projected statistics represent a player's projected major-league performance.

Below the projections are the player's three highest-scoring comparable players as determined by PECOTA. All comparables represent a snapshot of how the listed player was performing at the same age as the current player, so if a

23-year-old pitcher is compared to Bartolo Colón, he's actually being compared to a 23-year-old Colón, not the version that pitched for the Rangers in 2018, nor to Colón's career as a whole.

A few points about pitcher projections. First, we aren't yet projecting peak velocity, so that column will be blank in the PECOTA lines. Second, projecting DRA is trickier than evaluating past performance, because it is unclear how deserving each pitcher will be of his anticipated outcomes. However, we know that another DRA-related statistic–contextual FIP or cFIP-estimates future run scoring very well. So for PECOTA, the projected DRA figures you see are based on the past cFIPs generated by the pitcher and comparable players over time, along with the other factors described above.

Lineouts

In each chapter's Lineouts section, you'll find abbreviated text comments, as well as all the same information you'd find in our full player comments. The only difference is that we limit the stats boxes in this section to only including the 2019 information for each player.

Managers

After all those wonderful team chapters, we've got statistics for each big-league manager, all of whom are organized by alphabetical order. Here you'll find a block including an extraordinary amount of information collected from each manager's entire career. For more information on the acronyms and what they mean, please visit the Glossary at www.baseballprospectus.com.

There is one important metric that we'd like to call attention to, and you'll find it next to each manager's name: **wRM+** (weighted reliever management plus). Developed by Rob Arthur and Rian Watt, wRM+ investigates how good a manager is at using their best relievers during the moments of highest leverage, using both our proprietary DRA metric as well as Leverage Index. wRM+ is scaled to a league average of 100, and a wRM+ of 105 indicates that relievers were used approximately five percent "better" than average. On the other hand, a wRM+ of 95 would tell us the team used its relievers five percent "worse" than the average team.

While wRM+ does not have an extremely strong correlation with a manager, it is statistically significant; this means that a manager is not *entirely* responsible for a team's wRM+, but does have some effect on that number.

PECOTA Leaderboards

If you're familiar with PECOTA, then you'll have noticed that the projection system often appears bullish on players coming off a bad year and bearish on players coming off a good year. (This is because the system weights several previous seasons, not just the most recent one.) In addition, we publish the 50th

San Francisco Giants 2020

percentile projections for each player–which is smack in the middle of the range of projected production—which tends to mean PECOTA stat lines don't often have extreme results like 40 home runs or 250 strikeouts in a given season. In essence, PECOTA doesn't project very many extreme seasons.

At the end of the book, we've ranked the top players at each position based on their PECOTA projections. This might help you visualize just how a given player's projection compares to that of their peers, so that even if a dramatic stat line isn't projected, you can still imagine how they stack up against the rest of the league.

Part 1: Team Analysis

San Francisco Giants: Where Are You Going, Where Have You Been?

Craig Brown, Alexis Collins and Matthew Trueblood

2019: What Went Right

Participation in the wild card race can is often predicated upon false hope. The Giants, who won 19 of 25 games in July, unexpectedly found themselves just two games back for the second spot—unexpectedly because they had gone 36-47 through the end of June. This may have changed fannish perceptions of their relative place in the 2019 NL galaxy, but they were competing with five other teams for that lone position in baseball's postseason tournament. A moment of elation may change what you see in the mirror, it may grant a frisson of hope, but it does nothing to alter those kinds of odds.

As you know, the Giants didn't make it. They didn't come close to making it. Perhaps it's odd to find that under the entry of "What Went Right," but while the team was busy punching above its weight class the front office wasn't lulled into a false sense of possibility. As the trade deadline approached, they used the opportunity to deal from the strongest component of their team, the relief corps. Mark Melancon was shipped to Atlanta for what was basically salary relief, removing the $14 million he's due to collect next season from the books. Sam Dyson went to Minnesota for three lottery tickets. Drew Pomeranz and Ray Black were dropped on Milwaukee in exchange for a "Next Ten" prospect, Mauricio Dubón. Damn the wild-card race, these were all good trades.

Among those who remained, Madison Bumgarner was finally healthy for a full season and remembered he is, indeed, Madison Bumgarner, or at least a reasonable facsimile thereof. He saw more action in 2019 than in each of the previous two seasons. His strikeout rate wasn't where it was when he was dominating the National League from 2012-2016, but at 8.8 per nine, it was just a tick off his career mark. He restored (transiently, as it turned out) his status as the ace of the rotation. Reliever Will Smith closed 34 victories, led the staff with a 2.84 DRA, and paced the bullpen with a 1.8 WARP.

Finding positives for the position players is more challenging. We know that Oracle is a difficult place to hit dingers, but would it hurt anyone to just get on base? Brandon Belt paced the squad with a .339 OBP and possessed a 106 DRC+, but has seen his slugging percentage declined for the fourth consecutive year. After a dreadful first season with the Giants, Evan Longoria bounced back with a 100 DRC+, his highest total since 2016. Pablo Sandoval and his 98 DRC+ and .507 slugging percentage was a nice comeback story short-circuited by injury and the dreaded Tommy John surgery. Acquired in an April trade with the Blue Jays, Kevin Pillar had a good offensive season by his standards and provided the Giants with average defense in center. Donovan Solano, Austin Slater, and Alex Dickerson all showed flickers of promise in small sample sizes.

Although Belt, Longoria, and Buster Posey had higher WARP totals, the star of the position players was rookie 28-year-old Mike Yastrzemski. Acquired from Baltimore at the end of spring training, Yaz opened the year in Triple-A and was promoted to the big club Memorial Day weekend. With Hall of Fame bloodlines, young Yastrzemski led the Giants with a 112 DRC+ in just over 411 plate appearances. Yazito played solid defense as well while alternating between the corners.

2019: What Went Wrong

Hey, it's not the 2019 Giants' fault they migrated to the West Coast along with the Dodgers some 60 years ago. Geography dictates they both play in the NL West. Who knew geography could be so cruel? Even without the Dodger juggernaut in place, San Francisco was never expected to contend. Indeed, our preseason PECOTA projections pegged the Giants for 73 wins and a last-place finish in the NL West. They exceeded those expectations, but when the bar was set so low to start, that's not really that much of an accomplishment.

We just make it simple in this section and point a finger at the entire offense. The Giants managed just 4.19 runs per game, ranking ahead of only the Marlins on the circuit. The same goes for their .302 team OBP and .392 slugging percentage. Their cumulative DRC+ of 83 was, likewise, the second-worst in the league.

Buster Posey, who underwent hip surgery in August of 2018, struggled in his recovery, posting career lows in batting average (.257), OBP (.320), and slugging (.368). Shortstop Brandon Crawford stumbled to his worst offensive performance since 2012 and saw his once stellar defense decline. Belt bought into the launch angle revolution, hitting more fly balls than at any time in his career, but saw his HR/FB rate crater to around seven percent—and close to five percent at Oracle. He has yet to hit 20 home runs in a season.

The Giants just couldn't find adequate replacements for departed free agents Hunter Pence and Andrew McCutchen. Their revolving corner-outfield door saw 13 players start a game in left field. Eleven started in right. Opening Day center fielder Steven Duggar struggled to a 61 DRC+ in 281 plate appearances before a shoulder injury ended his season early for the second consecutive year. Speaking of revolving doors, how about the entire roster? The Giants used 64 different players, a franchise record. Some of that is creditable in a sense, a testimony to Zaidi's aggressive search for solutions. More of it, though, suggests the desperation of that search, and how rarely the attempted solutions paid off.

We might also indict the starting rotation, Bumgarner excepted. San Francisco starters posted a 5.19 DRA to go along with a 4.77 ERA. Their 8.0 strikeouts per nine was the second-lowest rate in the NL. Like the Giant batters have the Marlins to thank for keeping them out of the cellar in several team offensive categories, Giant starting pitchers will be sending gift baskets to Colorado and Pittsburgh as a token of thanks for keeping them out last place in myriad pitching categories.

Despite the kudos lavished above for the Giants recognizing their true talent level at the trade deadline, it is also fair to note that they opted not to move Bumgarner (who had a limited no-trade clause, primarily to contenders) and Smith, both of whom subsequently departed as free agents. Perhaps the market never developed for either. Still, it felt like something of a missed opportunity for a club facing a continuing rebuild. —*Craig Brown*

Prospect Outlook

"Objects in the rearview mirror are closer than they appear" is the reassuring lesson of 2019 down on the Giants' farm; for the first time in a few years, the Giants have some guys on the horizon that could be ready to help them as early as next season. A trio of prospects were called up to Double-A Richmond for the final month of the season, giving the organization a preview of what should be the next crop of talent. The 2018 number two overall pick **Joey Bart**, one of the youngest prospects in baseball, **Heliot Ramos**, and 6-foot-11 right-hander **Sean Hjelle** all have tools the Giants need sooner rather than later. Bart could make his way to the majors before the end of next season; Ramos and Hjelle are expected to need a bit more time before they are ready for the majors.

Top pitching prospect **Logan Webb** was suspended for 80 games after testing positive for PEDs, but he finished the season in the major league rotation. The former high school quarterback's limited repertoire may ultimately land him in the bullpen. While minor-league championships don't equate to major-league rings the Giants Triple-A team won the PCL title with another one of their pitching prospects, RHP **Melvin Adon**. Adon started the season in Double-A where he refined his slider and was named an all-star before earning a promotion to Triple-A. —*Alexis Collins*

San Francisco Giants 2020

2020 Outlook

Baseball is still a gigantic fraternity, in too many ways. Some of them were on full display this fall by the Bay. Zaidi hand-picked the man who would replace Bruce Bochy, after Bochy brought not only three championships but unfaltering dignity and decency to the Giants for a decade. Zaidi settled on Gabe Kapler, at least in part because of the time the two spent working closely together in the Dodgers front office. During that very period of collaboration, though, Kapler mishandled (and, ultimately, quashed) credible accusations of sexual assault made against players for whom he considered himself responsible. Those issues only came fully to light after Kapler got his job with the Phillies, but given that they're now public knowledge, and that Zaidi had ample opportunity to know more about the incidents earlier on, the fact that those issues went largely unaddressed during the hiring process was disquieting.

Zaidi then reinstated the position of general manager, a co-chief of baseball decisions who would answer directly to him and hired Scott Harris out of the Cubs' front office. Harris's previous claim to fame was that, during Chicago's run to the World Series title in 2016, others in the team's executive suite would urge him to eat entire loaves of bread when the team needed a rally. That the culture represented by the Giants' leadership group reflects those of so many tech companies in the Bay Area may make for neat narrative-building, but it sends mixed messages to the community of which the team is so much a part.

On the bright side, the team is thinking as progressively and as aggressively as those innovators and disruptors, too. They'll have 13 big-league coaches in 2020, the largest staff any team has ever carried. Included among them (though not one of the seven the league permits to be in uniform during games) will be Alyssa Nakken, an assistant focused on high performance and the first woman assigned a full-time coaching role with an MLB team. They're opening important avenues into the game as well as fully embracing a trend already sweeping the game: maximizing support, instruction, and development, to get the most out of as many players as possible. Their few on-field moves reflected the same objectives, though a different approach to them. Harris was part of the Cubs team that, while building toward their current competitive window, signed Paul Maholm, Scott Feldman, and Jason Hammel (among others who yielded less fruit). They then flipped all three for younger players who helped them get over the top. With that kind of arbitrage in mind, the Giants scooped up Kevin Gausman and Drew Smyly, two of the most attractive low-end starters on the market and claimed former Rockies lefty Tyler Anderson on waivers. If even one of them stays healthy and pitches the way they're able, San Francisco should be able to extract some measure of prospect punch for them in July. —*Matthew Trueblood*

Performance Graphs

2019 Hit List Ranking

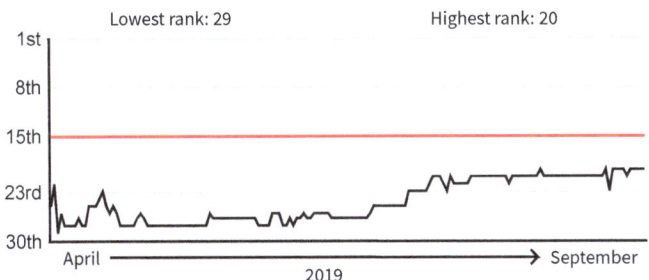

Committed Payroll (in millions)

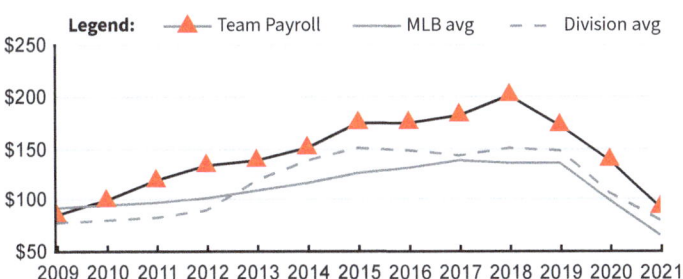

Farm System Ranking

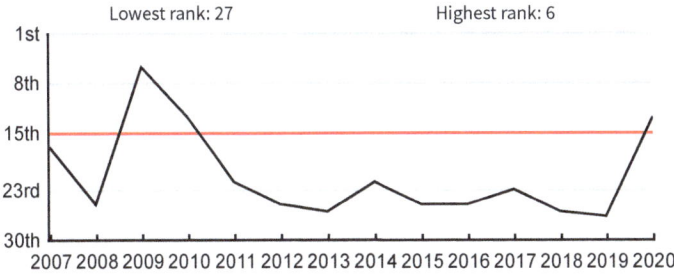

2019 Team Performance

ACTUAL STANDINGS

Team	W	L	Pct
LAN	106	56	0.654
ARI	85	77	0.525
SFN	**77**	**85**	**0.475**
COL	71	91	0.438
SDN	70	92	0.432

THIRD-ORDER STANDINGS

Team	W	L	Pct
LAN	114	48	0.702
ARI	84	78	0.516
SDN	74	88	0.454
SFN	**70**	**92**	**0.431**
COL	69	93	0.429

TOP HITTERS

Player	WARP
Buster Posey	2.7
Evan Longoria	2.6
Brandon Belt	1.9

TOP PITCHERS

Player	WARP
Madison Bumgarner	2.9
Jeff Samardzija	2.7
Will Smith	1.8

VITAL STATISTICS

Statistic Name	Value	Rank
Pythagenpat	.439	20th
Runs Scored per Game	4.19	28th
Runs Allowed per Game	4.77	16th
Deserved Runs Created Plus	83	28th
Deserved Run Average	5.03	20th
Fielding Independent Pitching	4.50	17th
Defensive Efficiency Rating	.713	7th
Batter Age	30.0	30th
Pitcher Age	28.9	23rd
Salary	$170.2M	6th
Marginal $ per Marginal Win	$5.5M	11th
Injured List Days	572	1st
$ on IL	13%	10th

2020 Team Projections

PROJECTED STANDINGS

Team	W	L	Pct	+/-
LAN	102.5	59.5	0.633	-4
SDN	79.3	82.7	0.490	9
ARI	78.9	83.1	0.487	-6
COL	76.6	85.4	0.473	6
SFN	**68.4**	**93.6**	**0.422**	**-9**

TOP PROJECTED HITTERS

Player	WARP
Buster Posey	2.6
Mike Yastrzemski	2.3
Brandon Belt	2.1

TOP PROJECTED PITCHERS

Player	WARP
Jeff Samardzija	1.4
Johnny Cueto	1.1
Kevin Gausman	1.1

FARM SYSTEM REPORT

Top Prospect	Number of Top 101 Prospects
Marco Luciano, #14	4

KEY DEDUCTIONS

Player	WARP
Madison Bumgarner	3.8
Will Smith	1.3
Stephen Vogt	0.1
Kevin Pillar	0.0
Burch Smith	-0.1

KEY ADDITIONS

Player	WARP
Kevin Gausman	1.1
Tyler Anderson	1.1
Hunter Pence	0.7
Wilmer Flores	0.7
Joey Bart	0.7
Darin Ruf	0.3
Yolmer Sánchez	0.2
Drew Smyly	0.2
Nick Vincent	0.2
Tyler Heineman	0.1

Team Personnel

President, Baseball Operations
Farhan Zaidi

Executive Vice President of Baseball Operations
Brian Sabean

General Manager
Scott Harris

Vice President of Baseball Operations
Yeshayah Goldfarb

Manager
Gabe Kapler

Oracle Park Stats

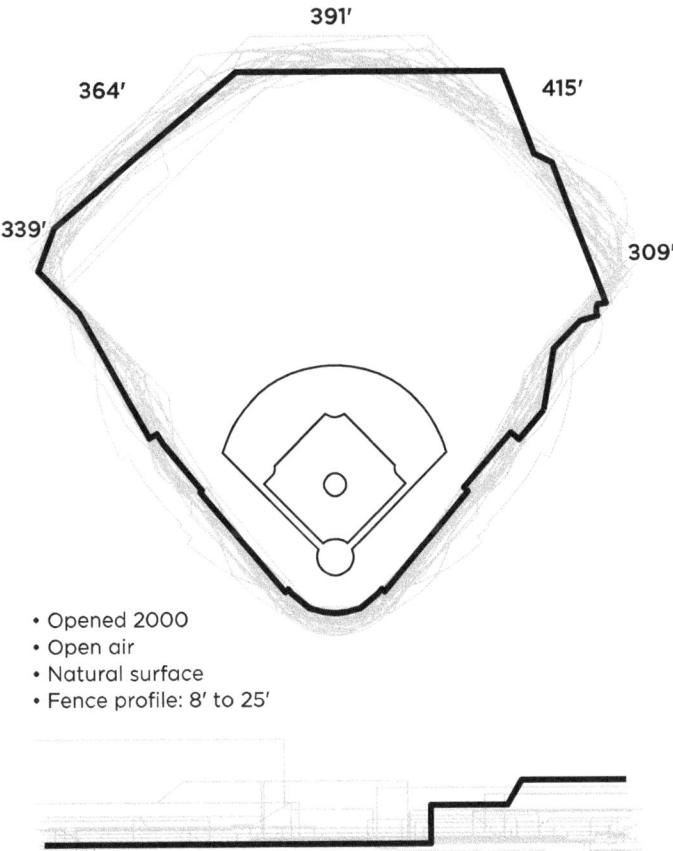

- Opened 2000
- Open air
- Natural surface
- Fence profile: 8' to 25'

Three-Year Park Factors

Runs	Runs/RH	Runs/LH	HR/RH	HR/LH
94	95	91	87	81

Giants Team Analysis

What is the difference between the San Francisco Giants and the Los Angeles Dodgers?

This is a dumb question.

Everything. The answer is everything. The Giants and Dodgers are complete opposites, and that opposition is, on the deepest particle level, what defines them, and it's been that way since the two franchises set out for California, hand-in-hand in the sunny spring of 1958. Hell, it may have been that way going back years earlier, to when they were sharing New York with the Yankees.

Manhattan and Brooklyn. San Francisco and LA. There are no Giants without Dodgers; there are no Dodgers without Giants. At least not like this. Black and orange. Pantone 294.

Just look at the previous decade. The Giants' story is one of highs and lows and inexplicable good vibes—of mediocrity punctuated by tremendous postseason success. Random misfits performing the feats of mythical heroes. Washed up Édgar Rentería and charmingly goofy Hunter Pence. A guy called, in all sincerity, Big Panda. The Giants' story is one of magic. The Dodgers' story, on the other hand, is one of cold and calculated and ruthless victory—and also, in that most crucial of ways—devastating futility.

I must confess here, that I was born and raised a Dodger fan. I once had a Coke thrown at me at Candlestick Park as a kid. But even I think it's good that things are this way. It's good that the Giants are the Giants and the Dodgers are the Dodgers. I wouldn't un-throw that Coke if I could. (I might send Alex Gordon in Game Seven of the 2014 World Series, though.)

One of the beautiful things about baseball is that every one of the 30 big league franchises has its own identity, and its own sensibility. But that version of the sport is fading away. We are entering a decade of same-ball. Of baseball by best practice. Thanks to the plentiful and increasing amount of data available to decision makers, everything from player evaluation practices to player development techniques is aligning. The search for an edge is becoming increasingly marginal, and increasingly distant from the actual game played on the field.

The Giants of the early 2010s did not play that version of baseball. They were all angles, and no launch. In fact, they may have been the last great weird-ball dynasty. But that era is over. You don't even have to squint. Bruce Bochy is gone. Madison Bumgarner has gone to Arizona to literally tend his horses. Even Buster

San Francisco Giants 2020

Posey is kind of just a guy now. The team's lack of success over the last five years might just have been one of those down cycles that even the greatest franchises can't avoid, it might just have been the result of a few bad breaks. Or maybe the Giants were getting left behind.

No longer. Before last season, the Giants hired Farhan Zaidi away from the Dodgers to run their baseball operations. Under Zaidi, they slowly began the process of remaking themselves as a hip, sleek data-driven franchise. They began to smooth out those angles. In some cases, this has been unceremonious. Joe Panik was quietly dismissed last August. Bochy was replaced by a man who seems, at least to relative outsiders, like his complete opposite in Gabe Kapler. But for the most part, the remaking of the Giants under Zaidi and his chosen general manager Scott Harris has been a quiet process.

To examine the list of transactions since Zaidi took office is the baseball equivalent of watching a time-lapse video of, like, a remote cliffside eroding over millennia. These transaction lists are their own form of quiet poetry. A roster gradually unmaking itself. The rhythmic crashing of waves, the rising and falling of tides, almost hypnotic in their smallness and their consistency. Aaron Altherr in and Aaron Altherr out. Tom Murphy in and Tom Murphy out. Hanser Alberto in and Hanser Alberto out. Yangervis Solarte. Connor Joe. Nick Vincent. Tyler Austin.

Jerry Dipoto has his trades. Farhan Zaidi has these quiet marginal moves. These tiny, intimate dramas. Sometimes the tides roll out. Sometimes you stumble on a Mike Yastrzemski. And in this way Zaidi has begun to unmake the Giants of Brian Sabean and Bobby Evans. Not in a sweeping way, but slowly, from the bottom up. One wave at a time until all that's left is Posey, standing on his tip toes, trying to keep his head above water.

The early offseason was more of the same. The Giants said goodbye to Bumgarner and Panda; to Bochy. They bought a nice prospect in Will Wilson by taking on the contract of injured Zack Cozart. This was exactly the kind of smart move that a wealthy franchise in a theoretical rebuilding state should be making. (By the way, even if he never plays a single inning in San Francisco Cozart is such a Giants guy.) But while it's a smart move, it's also a sort of clue. For the first time since before they signed Barry Bonds, the Giants franchise feels kind of small. This is not necessarily a bad thing—unless you're a Giants fan hoping for October glory right this minute.

They bring back a core of average-ish but established players. Joining Posey are Evan Longoria and Johnny Cueto and their contracts. Brandon Belt is still around, and for karmic reasons, it would be nice if he stayed healthy enough to enjoy the new dimensions at Oracle Park. Brandon Crawford is still around too, but barely. He was historically bad at the plate last year, and Kapler has already implied that he might not be an everyday player come 2020.

The rotation additions have been fine. Tyler Anderson and Kevin Gausman can and should eat innings alongside Cueto and Jeff Samardzija. They may even do a little better than that. Grant Brisbee, writing in The Athletic, implied that maybe Gausman could find his potential and morph into the next Jason Schmidt—and honestly, that seems plausible. There's upside!

But let's be honest, it would take a miracle for the Giants to actually compete. They are building toward some unspecified date in the future, when the coaching staff and player development apparatus are fully aligned, and that first wave of young controllable talent hits the big leagues. When they can become one of those unstoppable baseball machines with depth and maneuverability and players doing this and that. They are building toward becoming a Dodgers.

Even the manager they chose, Gabe Kapler, has his roots, like Zaidi, in the relatively recent Dodgers front office juggernaut. Before his short stint with the Phillies, Kapler was a player development director in LA, and the runner-up to Dave Roberts for that managerial opening after the 2015 season. Kapler comes with a bigger personality, and a more highly scrutinized history, than most managerial types. There's the lifestyle blog he had, there's the hyperenthusiastic personality, there's the embrace of nontraditional ideas (some of them are pretty normal; only in baseball would an executive be ridiculed for thinking it was a good idea for pro athletes to—gasp—eat healthy food); there's also the fact that he was accused of mishandling an assault case involving Dodger minor leaguers, and of firing Nick Francona for suffering from PTSD.

But if there *is* a miracle for the Giants, if they do compete ahead of schedule, it will probably have something to do with Kapler, and his, ahem, giant staff of coaches. The Giants will enter the season with at least three hitting coaches and three pitching coaches, including "pitching director" Brian Bannister who was lured away from the Red Sox. In his early interviews with San Francisco media, Kapler has stressed and restressed the idea of teaching at the major-league level. Those mediocre-to-solid old dudes who have been around forever don't necessarily have to stay mediocre or decline like we might expect them to; those fringe Zaidi pickups don't necessarily have to stay fringe. They may not all be Max Muncys, or even Mike Yastrzemskis—but they can contribute to a winning roster.

And this is it: a plausible, and somewhat interesting path forward for a franchise that has always seemed to find one; a successful end result of Zaidi's tinkering. The truth is, for all of the best practices they might share, and all their executive DNA they actually do share, it wouldn't be the worst thing for the Giants to start looking more like the Dodgers or vice versa; it would mean a competitive division year in and year out for the first time in a long time. It would mean a rivalry that pushes both teams to improve, to open their wallets, to nudge forward against whatever invisible forces are holding them back. Hell, it may force them to be creative, and find new ways to be different.

After all, these were the teams that brought baseball to the west coast. These were the teams that once upon a time, stretched the sport into its truly national form. The Giants never got the credit they deserved for that. But maybe the franchise that's been more stable than any—only 4 managers since 1993!—will be the one to shake things up.

—Eric Nusbaum is a freelance writer and former editor at VICE Sports.

Part 2: Player Analysis

PLAYER COMMENTS WITH GRAPHS

Brandon Belt 1B
Born: 04/20/88   Age: 32   Bats: L   Throws: L
Height: 6'4"   Weight: 235   Origin: Round 5, 2009 Draft (#147 overall)

YEAR	TEAM	LVL	AGE	PA	R	2B	3B	HR	RBI	BB	K	SB	CS	AVG/OBP/SLG
2017	SFN	MLB	29	451	63	27	3	18	51	66	104	3	2	.241/.355/.469
2018	SFN	MLB	30	456	50	18	2	14	46	49	107	4	0	.253/.342/.414
2019	SFN	MLB	31	616	76	32	3	17	57	83	127	4	3	.234/.339/.403
2020	SFN	MLB	32	602	66	25	4	17	67	78	135	5	3	.226/.332/.388

Comparables: Carlos Pena, Justin Smoak, Steve Balboni

Everything eventually comes full circle. After almost a decade of being one of the most divisive players in baseball (not to mention the Bay Area), Belt could be nearing the end of his complicated run with the Giants. Early in his career he spawned the hashtags #FreeBelt and #Belted as the representation of a shift in how to value a modern first baseman; possessed of only moderate power but excellent on-base skills, he was hardly the model of the hulking slugger, and it led the Giants to work him into the team much more tentatively than many fans wished. Once established, he produced but also suffered through a litany of injuries, most notably concussion-related symptoms that kept him from playing full seasons. In 2019 his offensive skills continued to gently wane, keeping him an above-average hitter but also a veteran on the periphery of an incoming youth movement. This year, his name will consistently come up in trade rumors, so once again we may see #FreeBelt applied, only this time he'll be off to a change in scenery.

YEAR	TEAM	LVL	AGE	PA	DRC+	VORP	BABIP	BRR	FRAA	WARP
2017	SFN	MLB	29	451	110	24.9	.284	0.3	1B(98): 9.0, LF(15): -0.3	2.1
2018	SFN	MLB	30	456	108	14.9	.311	-0.6	1B(104): 9.9, LF(8): 0.3	2.1
2019	SFN	MLB	31	616	106	14.8	.275	-2.2	1B(144): 7.2, LF(14): -0.5	1.9
2020	SFN	MLB	32	602	96	8.1	.273	-1.0	1B 11, LF 0	2.0

Brandon Belt, continued

Batted Ball Distribution

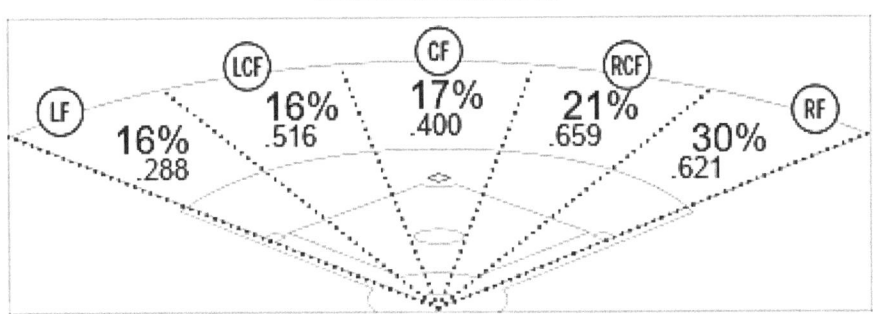

Strike Zone vs LHP	Strike Zone vs RHP
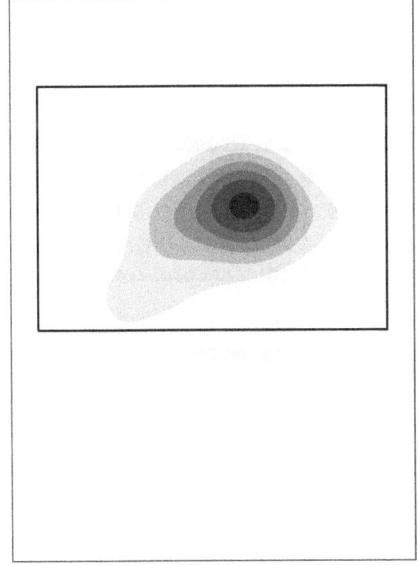	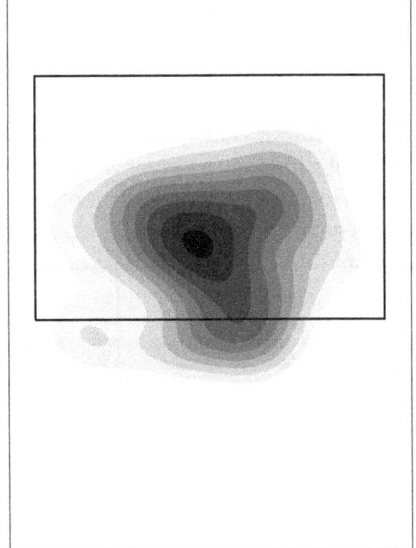

Zack Cozart 3B

Born: 08/12/85   Age: 34   Bats: R   Throws: R
Height: 6'0"   Weight: 205   Origin: Round 2, 2007 Draft (#79 overall)

YEAR	TEAM	LVL	AGE	PA	R	2B	3B	HR	RBI	BB	K	SB	CS	AVG/OBP/SLG
2017	CIN	MLB	31	507	80	24	7	24	63	62	78	3	0	.297/.385/.548
2018	LAA	MLB	32	253	29	13	2	5	18	19	42	0	0	.219/.296/.362
2019	LAA	MLB	33	107	4	2	0	0	7	5	16	0	0	.124/.178/.144
2020	SFN	MLB	34	112	11	5	1	3	12	8	20	1	0	.219/.287/.367

Comparables: Jordy Mercer, Brendan Ryan, Paul Janish

In 2017, Cozart may have had the contract year to end all contract years. After several steady-but-not-great seasons as the Reds' shortstop, Cozart caught that Joey Votto On-Base Fever, torqued it up with some long-ball power, and floated into free agency with the wind of a 4.5-win season beneath his wings. The Angels sidled up with a three-year deal, and shortly thereafter Cozart's shoulder decided to break down. It's hard to fly with a broken wing, and two surgeries later Cozart still hasn't taken flight. Even 2020 looks uncertain for the 34-year-old despite moving 400-odd miles north on I-5.

   It is tempting to see this turn of events as a knock on the Angels' front office and a reinforcement of the perils of free agency. Confirmation that Cozart's signing was a "mistake" or a "bad contract." Another way to view the contract, though: it's unlikely a player who averaged 122 games a year over the prior six seasons would accumulate fewer than 100 the next two. It's clear Cozart's injuries have compromised his play, and that was a bummer for the Angels and their fans alike, but we can also appreciate that the former second-round pick made good and cashed in before misfortune struck.

YEAR	TEAM	LVL	AGE	PA	DRC+	VORP	BABIP	BRR	FRAA	WARP
2017	CIN	MLB	31	507	137	50.5	.312	-2.8	SS(112): 1.3	4.5
2018	LAA	MLB	32	253	90	3.3	.244	-0.2		0.5
2019	LAA	MLB	33	107	66	-0.4	.143	0.4		-0.1
2020	SFN	MLB	34	112	76	-0.5	.246	-0.3	3B 0, 2B 0	-0.1

Zack Cozart, continued

Batted Ball Distribution

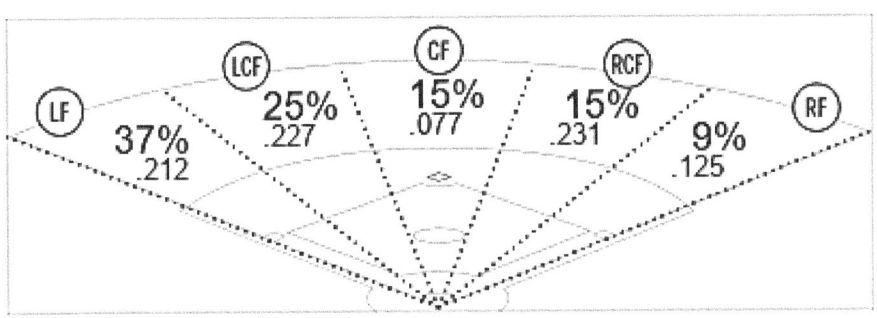

Strike Zone vs LHP   **Strike Zone vs RHP**

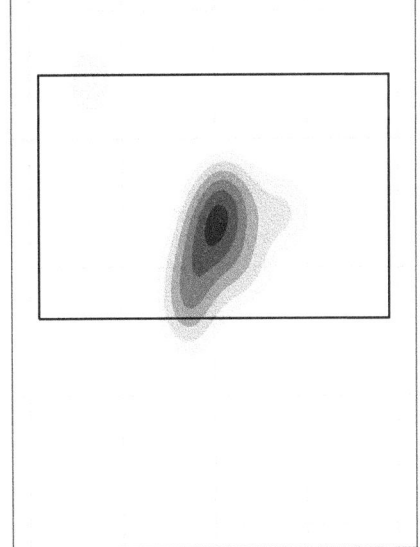

Brandon Crawford SS

Born: 01/21/87 Age: 33 Bats: L Throws: R
Height: 6'2" Weight: 227 Origin: Round 4, 2008 Draft (#117 overall)

YEAR	TEAM	LVL	AGE	PA	R	2B	3B	HR	RBI	BB	K	SB	CS	AVG/OBP/SLG
2017	SFN	MLB	30	570	58	34	1	14	77	42	113	3	5	.253/.305/.403
2018	SFN	MLB	31	594	63	28	2	14	54	50	122	4	5	.254/.325/.394
2019	SFN	MLB	32	560	58	24	2	11	59	53	117	3	2	.228/.304/.350
2020	*SFN*	*MLB*	*33*	*595*	*57*	*26*	*3*	*13*	*60*	*54*	*133*	*6*	*3*	*.230/.306/.363*

Comparables: Trevor Plouffe, Stephen Drew, Hanley Ramirez

The reputation as a "defense-only" player can be a double-edged sword. For years, people could only see his wizardry, his quickness, and a silky smooth transition from glove to rifle arm—it shaded the fact that he was an improving offensive player worthy even of a Silver Slugger award, despite his lackluster OBP. This past season, perhaps due to his 2018 knee injury or his advancing age, his defensive prowess has slipped and he graded out as an average defender for the first time in his career. It's possible his vaunted reputation—or the fact that he's being paid $30 million over the next two years—will continue to make him a regular in the Giants' infield despite his fading skills. More than likely, it's the reputation that once caused people to undervalue his stick which may save him from becoming a utility infielder or worse in 2020.

YEAR	TEAM	LVL	AGE	PA	DRC+	VORP	BABIP	BRR	FRAA	WARP
2017	SFN	MLB	30	570	84	23.6	.293	-1.4	SS(138): 4.1	1.7
2018	SFN	MLB	31	594	95	27.1	.303	0.5	SS(146): 15.3	4.0
2019	SFN	MLB	32	560	80	12.2	.274	-3.4	SS(142): 0.9	0.9
2020	*SFN*	*MLB*	*33*	*595*	*80*	*6.6*	*.284*	*-0.6*	*SS 1*	*0.8*

Brandon Crawford, continued

Batted Ball Distribution

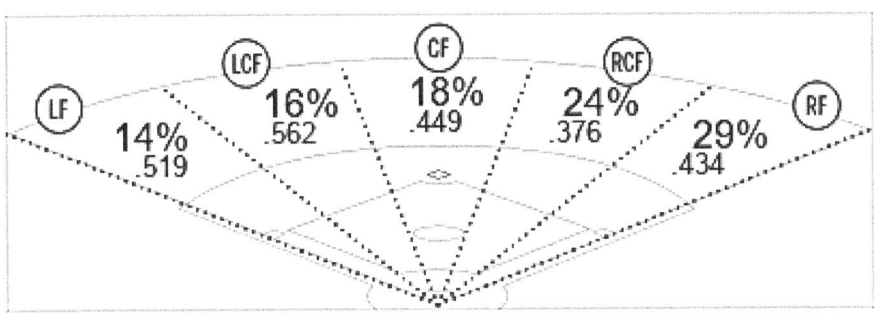

Strike Zone vs LHP   Strike Zone vs RHP

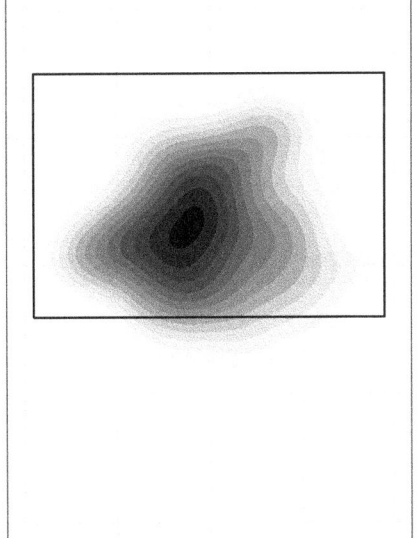

San Francisco Giants 2020

Jaylin Davis RF
Born: 07/01/94 Age: 25 Bats: R Throws: R
Height: 6'1" Weight: 190 Origin: Round 24, 2015 Draft (#710 overall)

YEAR	TEAM	LVL	AGE	PA	R	2B	3B	HR	RBI	BB	K	SB	CS	AVG/OBP/SLG
2017	CDR	A	22	272	36	13	3	12	41	16	77	9	2	.267/.316/.486
2017	FTM	A+	22	233	26	8	2	3	25	12	70	1	1	.237/.288/.335
2018	FTM	A+	23	227	23	10	0	5	19	23	57	3	2	.271/.354/.397
2018	CHT	AA	23	267	30	14	2	6	34	21	69	5	2	.275/.341/.425
2019	PEN	AA	24	251	34	9	0	10	25	36	64	7	3	.274/.382/.458
2019	ROC	AAA	24	173	39	11	1	15	42	15	46	2	0	.331/.405/.708
2019	SAC	AAA	24	117	21	6	0	10	27	14	28	1	1	.333/.419/.686
2019	SFN	MLB	24	47	2	0	0	1	3	3	11	1	2	.167/.255/.238
2020	SFN	MLB	26	105	11	4	0	4	12	9	34	1	0	.222/.296/.381

Comparables: Brad Komminsk, Aaron Altherr, Johnny Lewis

From an oft-injured afterthought to a key piece in a deadline deal, Davis had a revelatory 2019, finally able to stay healthy and tap into his raw power. He launched dinger after dinger, no matter the minor-league level or organization, finishing the year with 35 minor-league bombs and a single emphatic walk-off homer in the big leagues to put an exclamation point on his year. It wasn't all home run trots and walk-off celebrations for him, as much of his debut consisted of ground ball outs, and he's still not rocketing up prospect lists ... but another hot start in Triple-A might force the issue and make the Giants push him into the big leagues for another chance to make a first impression.

YEAR	TEAM	LVL	AGE	PA	DRC+	VORP	BABIP	BRR	FRAA	WARP
2017	CDR	A	22	272	105	13.6	.335	1.1	RF(60): 7.4	1.5
2017	FTM	A+	22	233	65	-6.0	.333	-0.5	RF(45): 4.4, LF(10): 2.3	0.3
2018	FTM	A+	23	227	126	12.4	.355	4.1	RF(50): -6.2, LF(2): -0.2	0.7
2018	CHT	AA	23	267	111	7.9	.359	-0.2	RF(50): 2.5, CF(1): -0.1	1.1
2019	PEN	AA	24	251	156	18.3	.345	-0.2	RF(42): -2.0, LF(8): 0.8	1.8
2019	ROC	AAA	24	173	160	19.0	.387	0.3	RF(32): 2.8, CF(6): 0.5	1.8
2019	SAC	AAA	24	117	138	13.6	.375	0.9	RF(15): 3.1, CF(7): 0.6	1.2
2019	SFN	MLB	24	47	68	-0.8	.200	-0.7	RF(15): -0.5	-0.2
2020	SFN	MLB	26	105	83	-0.3	.304	-0.2	RF 0	-0.1

Jaylin Davis, continued

Batted Ball Distribution

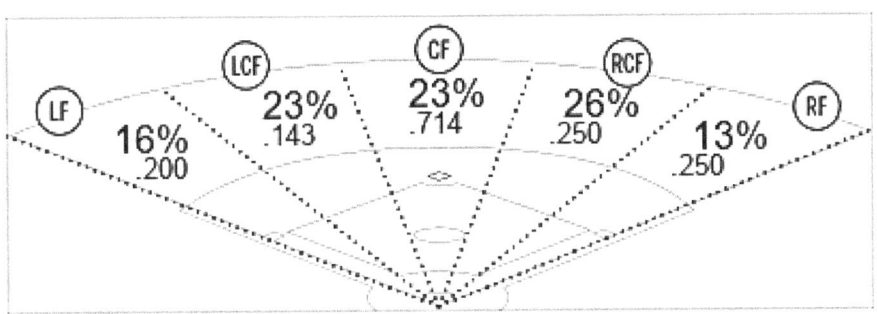

Strike Zone vs LHP

Strike Zone vs RHP

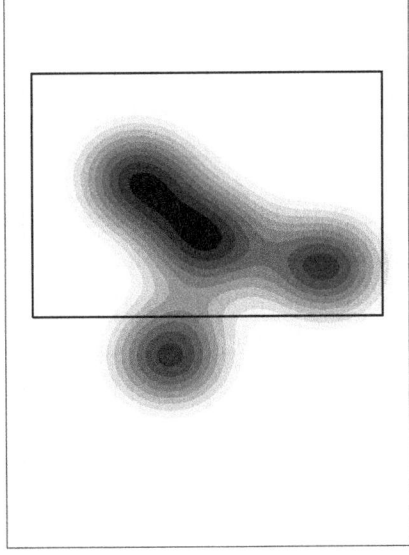

Alex Dickerson LF

Born: 05/26/90 Age: 30 Bats: L Throws: L
Height: 6'3" Weight: 235 Origin: Round 3, 2011 Draft (#91 overall)

YEAR	TEAM	LVL	AGE	PA	R	2B	3B	HR	RBI	BB	K	SB	CS	AVG/OBP/SLG
2019	ELP	AAA	29	113	17	5	1	5	20	14	18	0	0	.372/.469/.606
2019	SDN	MLB	29	19	1	0	0	0	2	0	7	0	0	.158/.158/.158
2019	SFN	MLB	29	171	28	13	3	6	26	13	35	1	1	.290/.351/.529
2020	SFN	MLB	30	336	36	17	3	10	39	26	75	2	1	.253/.323/.422

Comparables: John Mayberry Jr., Seth Smith, Allen Craig

Two years off the field can be a lifetime, especially when you're establishing yourself as a major-league regular. But after recovering from back and elbow injuries, Dickerson returned to the majors with a vengeance last year, and was a major catalyst for the Giants' lineup through June and July. From a mid-season bit of transactional fluff to a regular role in the outfield, he promptly hit a grand slam in his first game with the Giants, and was one of the premier hitters in baseball—so long as the opposing pitcher was right-handed—right up until the time that the injury bug crept up again and hampered his performance as the season wore down. Nevertheless, Dickerson has proven that he could have serious value as a left-handed bat, as long as he's handled with kid gloves and not relied on to play 150 games a season. As a complement to the Austin Slaters of the world, he could likely outperform his $1.2 million contract for 2020.

YEAR	TEAM	LVL	AGE	PA	DRC+	VORP	BABIP	BRR	FRAA	WARP
2019	ELP	AAA	29	113	126	10.1	.417	0.6	1B(6): -0.5, LF(6): 0.3	0.7
2019	SDN	MLB	29	19	67	-0.2	.250	0.2	LF(6): -0.1	0.0
2019	SFN	MLB	29	171	104	5.7	.339	0.5	LF(44): -4.5, RF(1): -0.2	0.1
2020	SFN	MLB	30	336	100	9.4	.307	0.1	LF -1	0.8

Alex Dickerson, continued

Batted Ball Distribution

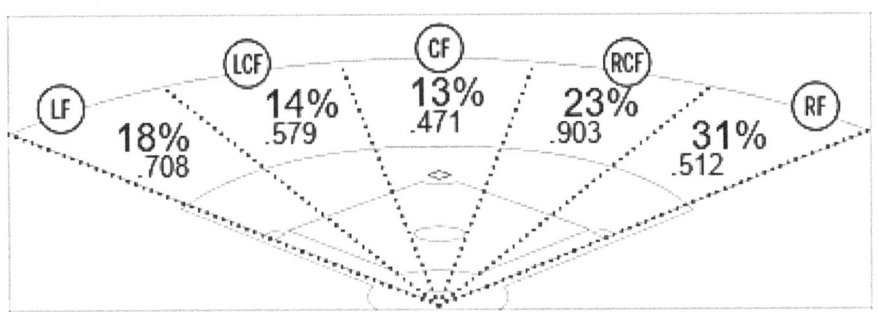

| Strike Zone vs LHP | Strike Zone vs RHP |

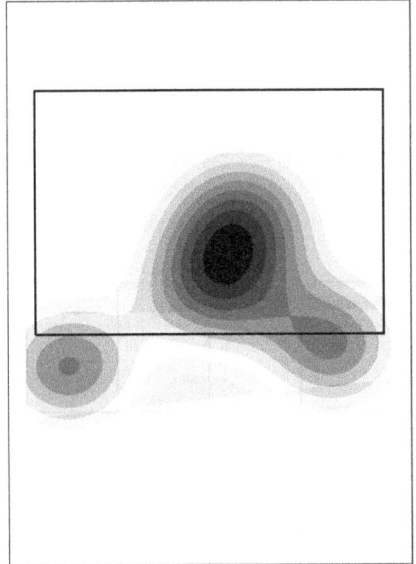 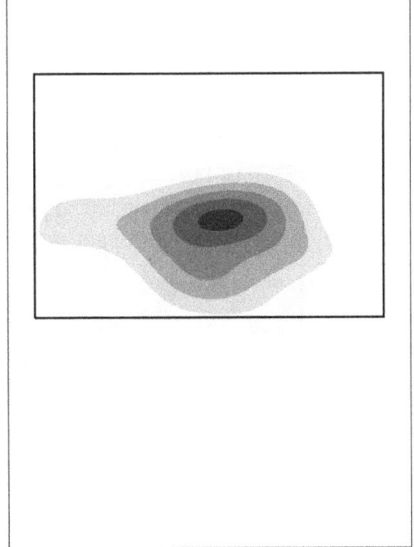

San Francisco Giants 2020

Mauricio Dubón SS

Born: 07/19/94   Age: 25   Bats: R   Throws: R
Height: 6'0"   Weight: 160   Origin: Round 26, 2013 Draft (#773 overall)

YEAR	TEAM	LVL	AGE	PA	R	2B	3B	HR	RBI	BB	K	SB	CS	AVG/OBP/SLG
2017	BLX	AA	22	304	34	14	0	2	24	25	42	31	9	.276/.338/.351
2017	CSP	AAA	22	244	40	15	0	6	33	14	34	7	6	.272/.320/.420
2018	CSP	AAA	23	114	18	9	2	4	18	2	19	6	3	.343/.348/.574
2019	SAN	AAA	24	427	59	22	1	16	47	18	59	9	6	.297/.333/.475
2019	SAC	AAA	24	112	23	4	0	4	9	10	9	1	2	.323/.391/.485
2019	SFN	MLB	24	109	12	5	0	4	9	5	19	3	1	.279/.312/.442
2019	MIL	MLB	24	2	0	0	0	0	0	0	1	0	0	.000/.000/.000
2020	SFN	MLB	25	385	37	15	1	9	40	18	68	13	4	.250/.290/.375

Comparables: Yairo Muñoz, Marwin Gonzalez, Didi Gregorius

Stop me if you've heard this one before, but it looks like a high-contact hitter with a solid defensive reputation may be stepping into the No. 2 spot in the order and the second base job with the Giants next year. After a solid start to his Giants career (and four homers in 109 plate appearances), Dubón might be an upgrade over the dear-but-departed Joe Panik. With Gabe Kapler manning the lineups instead of Bruce Bochy, it's likely that this solid-fielding rookie middle infielder will get first crack at the everyday second base job over the likes of Donovan Solano, but if there's a lack of power or consistency, Dubón is a perfect fit for a 2B/SS/CF utility role while providing offense against lefties. Entering his age-25 season and with little left to prove in the minors, it's finally time for MLB's first Honduran-born player to get an everyday role.

YEAR	TEAM	LVL	AGE	PA	DRC+	VORP	BABIP	BRR	FRAA	WARP
2017	BLX	AA	22	304	101	6.0	.319	0.3	SS(53): 5.4, 2B(20): 3.0	2.3
2017	CSP	AAA	22	244	76	0.4	.297	-0.4	SS(30): -1.0, 2B(27): 3.5	0.4
2018	CSP	AAA	23	114	107	10.6	.379	1.5	SS(23): 0.3, 2B(4): 0.6	0.8
2019	SAN	AAA	24	427	103	22.9	.316	-0.9	SS(83): 4.1, 2B(12): 0.7	2.4
2019	SAC	AAA	24	112	103	8.4	.326	0.6	SS(17): -0.1, 2B(6): 0.3	0.9
2019	SFN	MLB	24	109	88	2.4	.309	1.1	2B(22): 3.8, SS(9): -0.4	0.7
2019	MIL	MLB	24	2	84	0.1	.000	0.0	SS(1): 0.0	0.0
2020	SFN	MLB	25	385	78	4.5	.286	0.4	2B 9, SS 0	1.5

Mauricio Dubón, continued

Batted Ball Distribution

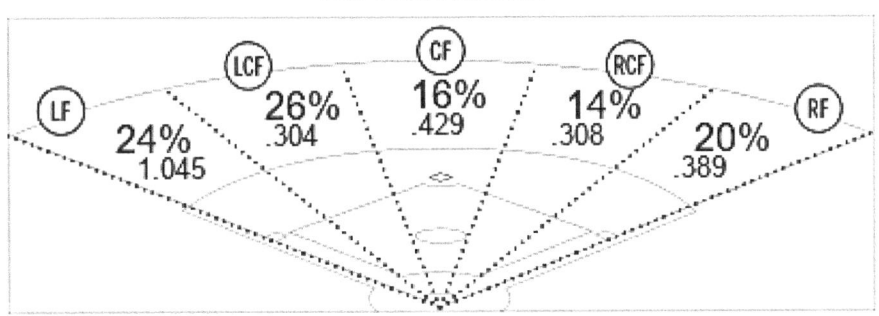

Strike Zone vs LHP   Strike Zone vs RHP

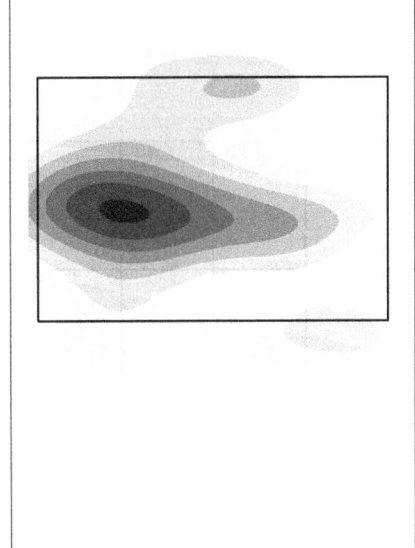

San Francisco Giants 2020

Steven Duggar RF
Born: 11/04/93   Age: 26   Bats: L   Throws: R
Height: 6'2"   Weight: 189   Origin: Round 6, 2015 Draft (#186 overall)

YEAR	TEAM	LVL	AGE	PA	R	2B	3B	HR	RBI	BB	K	SB	CS	AVG/OBP/SLG
2017	SJO	A+	23	133	22	11	0	4	20	17	42	7	0	.270/.361/.470
2017	SAC	AAA	23	54	7	1	0	2	6	8	12	3	2	.261/.370/.413
2018	SAC	AAA	24	356	52	27	4	4	21	39	103	11	4	.272/.354/.421
2018	SFN	MLB	24	152	20	11	1	2	17	10	44	5	1	.255/.303/.390
2019	SAC	AAA	25	102	24	6	1	3	13	18	21	2	3	.337/.461/.542
2019	SFN	MLB	25	281	26	12	2	4	28	16	78	1	4	.234/.278/.341
2020	SFN	MLB	26	490	44	20	3	8	45	42	134	8	4	.229/.299/.340

Comparables: Bradley Zimmer, Kirk Nieuwenhuis, Chad Hermansen

On Opening Day, Duggar was "the promising one" out of the Giants' makeshift outfield crop. Flanked by Connor Joe and Michael Reed, Duggar stood out as the one player on the grass with a real possibility to be more than just a piece of Sporcle trivia in a few years. When the team acquired Kevin Pillar in April—a player who would've made Duggar redundant on most outfield depth charts—he moved to right field but battled back injuries and ineffectiveness at the plate before suffering a shoulder strain that will keep him rehabbing until spring training. There's still some potential that he can be the center of San Francisco's outfield, but now it seems as if he's merely the answer to the trivia question "Who played center field for the Giants before Heliot Ramos got called up?"

YEAR	TEAM	LVL	AGE	PA	DRC+	VORP	BABIP	BRR	FRAA	WARP
2017	SJO	A+	23	133	130	9.7	.386	2.0	RF(22): -2.3, CF(1): -0.2	0.6
2017	SAC	AAA	23	54	95	3.0	.313	0.1	CF(12): 1.7	0.3
2018	SAC	AAA	24	356	103	13.1	.392	-0.1	CF(74): 9.6	2.4
2018	SFN	MLB	24	152	71	8.3	.354	3.6	CF(40): -3.4	0.0
2019	SAC	AAA	25	102	138	13.1	.424	0.2	CF(19): 0.4	0.9
2019	SFN	MLB	25	281	61	-5.6	.313	-1.4	CF(39): 2.1, RF(34): -0.8	-0.6
2020	SFN	MLB	26	490	73	1.7	.310	1.5	CF 7, RF -1	0.9

Steven Duggar, continued

Batted Ball Distribution

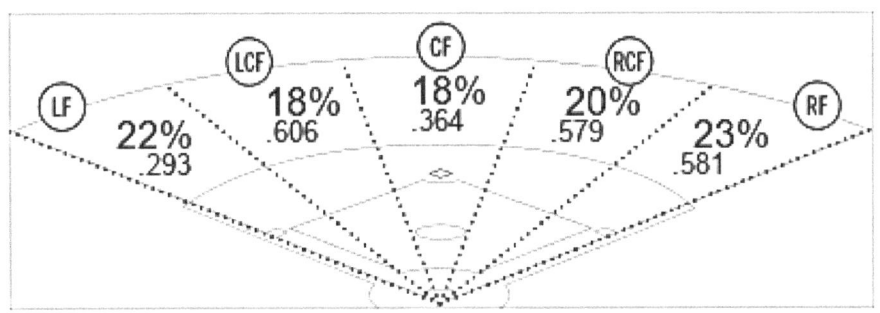

Strike Zone vs LHP   Strike Zone vs RHP

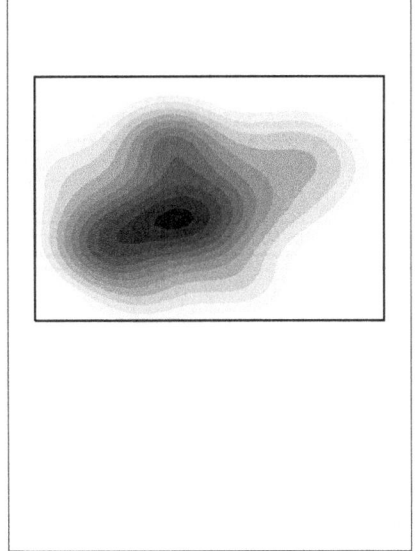

Wilmer Flores INF

Born: 08/06/91 Age: 28 Bats: R Throws: R
Height: 6'3" Weight: 205 Origin: International Free Agent, 2007

YEAR	TEAM	LVL	AGE	PA	R	2B	3B	HR	RBI	BB	K	SB	CS	AVG/OBP/SLG
2017	NYN	MLB	25	362	42	17	1	18	52	17	54	1	1	.271/.307/.488
2018	NYN	MLB	26	429	43	25	0	11	51	29	42	0	0	.267/.319/.417
2019	ARI	MLB	27	285	31	18	0	9	37	15	31	0	0	.317/.361/.487
2020	ARI	MLB	28	251	29	12	0	10	33	14	34	1	0	.270/.317/.448

Comparables: Cal Ripken Jr., Jay Bell, Jim Fregosi

Flores hit well in his part-time role with the Diamondbacks, spelling Christian Walker at first base and playing second when Ketel Marte was in center. He also got hurt, missing about two months with a broken foot. He was a poor defender at both spots, and it turns out breaking a foot doesn't help one's already declining defensive prowess. Flores would likely be better served playing for an American League club where he can primarily DH and play the field in a pinch. It's not clear that his bat can justify that type of role without the BABIP-infused progress it made in 2019. Somehow just 28, Flores feels more like he's exiting his prime than entering it.

YEAR	TEAM	LVL	AGE	PA	DRC+	VORP	BABIP	BRR	FRAA	WARP
2017	NYN	MLB	25	362	112	15.8	.270	-0.6	3B(55): 0.2, 1B(29): -0.2	1.5
2018	NYN	MLB	26	429	106	13.3	.269	-3.2	1B(83): -2.6, 2B(13): 0.1	0.4
2019	ARI	MLB	27	285	117	15.5	.332	-0.2	2B(64): -5.4, 1B(16): 0.1	1.0
2020	ARI	MLB	28	251	100	7.4	.281	-0.7	1B 0, 2B -1	0.6

Wilmer Flores, continued

Batted Ball Distribution

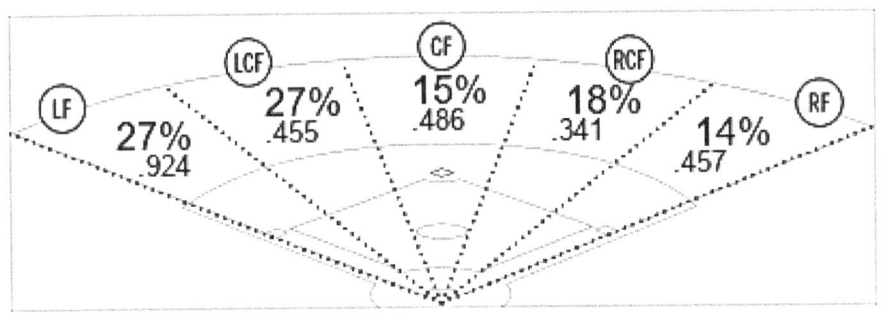

Strike Zone vs LHP   Strike Zone vs RHP

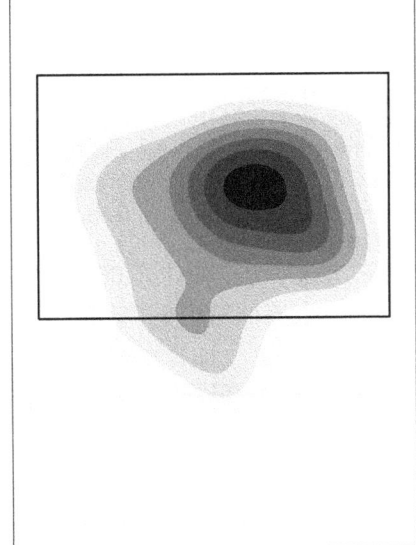

Aramis Garcia C
Born: 01/12/93 Age: 27 Bats: R Throws: R
Height: 6'2" Weight: 220 Origin: Round 2, 2014 Draft (#52 overall)

YEAR	TEAM	LVL	AGE	PA	R	2B	3B	HR	RBI	BB	K	SB	CS	AVG/OBP/SLG
2017	SJO	A+	24	347	43	20	1	17	65	15	73	0	0	.272/.314/.497
2017	RIC	AA	24	89	11	12	0	0	8	9	21	0	0	.282/.360/.436
2018	RIC	AA	25	328	36	14	1	11	33	20	76	0	1	.233/.287/.395
2018	SAC	AAA	25	41	5	1	0	0	4	2	12	0	0	.237/.268/.263
2018	SFN	MLB	25	65	8	1	0	4	9	2	31	0	0	.286/.308/.492
2019	SAC	AAA	26	371	52	20	2	16	55	34	114	0	2	.271/.343/.488
2019	SFN	MLB	26	46	5	1	0	2	5	4	21	0	0	.143/.217/.310
2020	SFN	MLB	27	322	30	12	1	10	35	21	117	0	0	.210/.268/.354

Comparables: Grayson Greiner, Michael Perez, Lane Adams

At the risk of sounding like an amateur real estate agent, might we suggest Garcia invest in a home somewhere in Fairfield, or maybe Rio Vista? A cottage evenly set between San Francisco and Sacramento is the perfect spot for the team's likely third catcher, who should split time between Triple-A and the bigs in 2020. With only two dozen hits sprinkled across cups of coffee in two seasons, the FIU product hasn't yet translated his solid minor-league performance into acceptable lines in the majors. Even at 27, there's still some hope that he can align his strengths and shore up his weaknesses enough to be a solid regular, but until then he'll hang his hat in the spaces between.

YEAR	TEAM	P. COUNT	FRM RUNS	BLK RUNS	THRW RUNS	TOT RUNS
2017	RIC	2761	-0.4	0.2	-0.1	-0.7
2018	RIC	9457	13.6	-0.6	-1.5	11.3
2018	SAC	1487	-0.2	0.0	0.0	0.3
2018	SFN	874	0.4	0.3	0.0	0.7
2019	SAC	9165	3.7	-0.1	1.8	5.2
2019	SFN	1465	1.5	-1.0	0.0	0.5
2020	SFN	10438	7.9	-1.5	0.4	6.8

YEAR	TEAM	LVL	AGE	PA	DRC+	VORP	BABIP	BRR	FRAA	WARP
2017	SJO	A+	24	347	115	20.8	.301	-1.3	C(50): 0.7, 1B(17): 0.3	1.7
2017	RIC	AA	24	89	120	6.5	.379	1.0	C(20): -0.5, 1B(2): 0.0	0.7
2018	RIC	AA	25	328	92	10.4	.272	-2.0	C(69): 10.3, 1B(11): -0.5	2.0
2018	SAC	AAA	25	41	62	-1.6	.333	0.3	C(10): 0.5	0.1
2018	SFN	MLB	25	65	55	3.0	.500	0.2	1B(10): -0.6, C(7): 0.7	-0.2
2019	SAC	AAA	26	371	89	14.6	.365	0.0	C(60): 6.6, 1B(23): -1.4	1.5
2019	SFN	MLB	26	46	56	-0.7	.211	0.2	C(11): 0.8, 1B(5): 0.5	0.1
2020	SFN	MLB	27	322	67	-0.3	.308	-0.5	C 7, 1B 0	0.6

Aramis Garcia, continued

Batted Ball Distribution

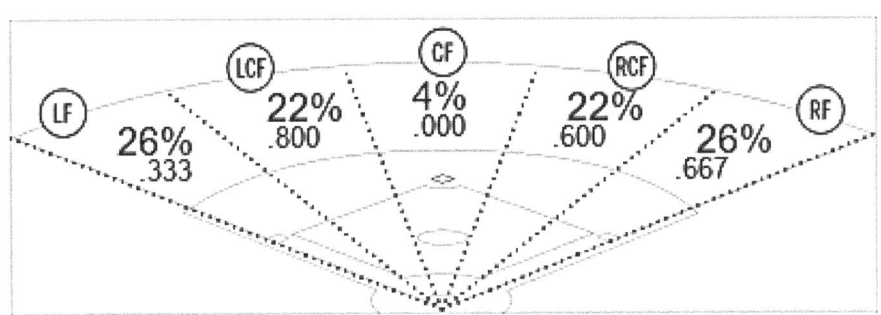

Strike Zone vs LHP

Strike Zone vs RHP

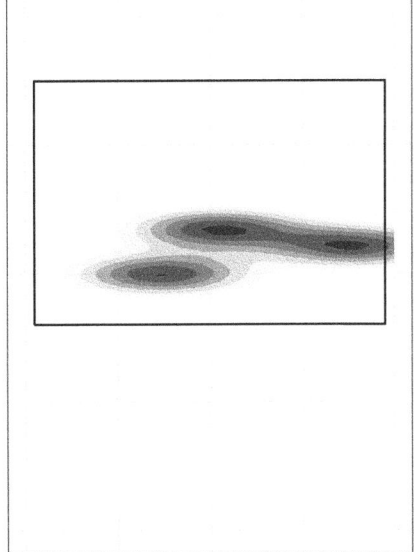

San Francisco Giants 2020

Billy Hamilton CF
Born: 09/09/90   Age: 29   Bats: B   Throws: R
Height: 6'0"   Weight: 160   Origin: Round 2, 2009 Draft (#57 overall)

YEAR	TEAM	LVL	AGE	PA	R	2B	3B	HR	RBI	BB	K	SB	CS	AVG/OBP/SLG
2017	CIN	MLB	26	633	85	17	11	4	38	44	133	59	13	.247/.299/.335
2018	CIN	MLB	27	556	74	16	9	4	29	46	132	34	10	.236/.299/.327
2019	ATL	MLB	28	48	9	2	0	0	3	7	13	4	1	.268/.375/.317
2019	KCA	MLB	28	305	32	12	2	0	12	25	74	18	5	.211/.275/.269
2020	ATL	MLB	29	251	22	8	2	3	19	20	62	21	5	.218/.281/.301

Comparables: Brian McRae, Dave Martinez, Jerome Walton

For most games at SunTrust Park, a local sprinter known as "The Freeze" takes on a random fan from that night's Braves game in a foot race where the fan gets a head start. This normally results in The Freeze still taking the victory, but there was finally some intrigue about The Freeze getting a formidable opponent once the Braves traded for Hamilton. The race never happened during the 2019 season, so Atlanta had to settle for Hamilton coming off the bench to deliver blazing speed and capable defense when needed. Those two attributes are just about all you're going to get from Hamilton at this point, as it's clear that he's never going to do enough damage at the plate to be considered a real threat with the bat. Still, the advent of the 26th roster spot increases the chances that there is a place for Hamilton and the two definitive things he offers—well, three if you include potential between-innings hijinks.

YEAR	TEAM	LVL	AGE	PA	DRC+	VORP	BABIP	BRR	FRAA	WARP
2017	CIN	MLB	26	633	66	4.2	.313	6.6	CF(137): 5.1	0.7
2018	CIN	MLB	27	556	70	8.5	.309	8.3	CF(150): 4.2	1.2
2019	ATL	MLB	28	48	83	0.7	.393	0.5	CF(24): -2.7	-0.2
2019	KCA	MLB	28	305	56	-6.4	.286	4.0	CF(90): -2.9	-0.5
2020	ATL	MLB	29	251	55	-3.9	.286	2.6	CF 0	-0.4

Billy Hamilton, continued

Batted Ball Distribution

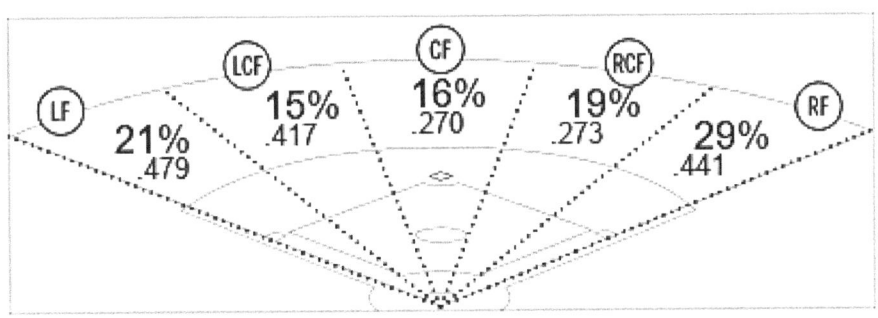

Strike Zone vs LHP   **Strike Zone vs RHP**

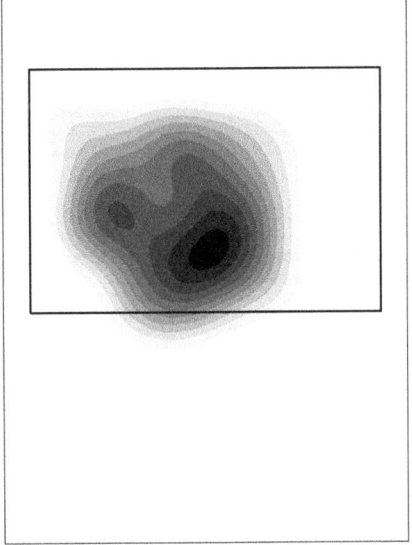

Evan Longoria 3B

Born: 10/07/85 Age: 34 Bats: R Throws: R
Height: 6'1" Weight: 215 Origin: Round 1, 2006 Draft (#3 overall)

YEAR	TEAM	LVL	AGE	PA	R	2B	3B	HR	RBI	BB	K	SB	CS	AVG/OBP/SLG
2017	TBA	MLB	31	677	71	36	2	20	86	46	109	6	1	.261/.313/.424
2018	SFN	MLB	32	512	51	25	4	16	54	22	101	3	1	.244/.281/.413
2019	SFN	MLB	33	508	59	19	2	20	69	43	112	3	1	.254/.325/.437
2020	SFN	MLB	34	567	61	27	2	19	68	42	130	3	1	.244/.308/.412

Comparables: Eric Chavez, Mike Pagliarulo, Edwin Encarnación

Four years ago, this *Annual* compared Longoria's career to Joseph Campbell's monomyth, the hero's journey. Over the course of his career, the veteran third baseman overcame many trials, from being forced to play in the Trop to watching his skillset diminish with age, but none were as haunting as what he faced in his first season in San Francisco, an unmitigated disaster wherein both his defense and his patience evaporated. For a moment, it seemed as if this journey would never be completed, that he would fall into the abyss, and never receive his ultimate boon, be that a World Series ring or a call to the Hall of Fame. But while the future is yet unwritten, the 34-year-old still drives towards his apotheosis. Last year he was the Giants' second-best hitter among regulars, and his FRAA bounced back from his dismal 2018 numbers. It might be hard to see Longoria reaching the pinnacle of his journey wearing the orange and brown of a mid-tier Giants team, but the end of the journey has not come yet, and the end of his story is yet to be told.

YEAR	TEAM	LVL	AGE	PA	DRC+	VORP	BABIP	BRR	FRAA	WARP
2017	TBA	MLB	31	677	95	22.2	.282	-1.9	3B(142): 3.8	2.1
2018	SFN	MLB	32	512	89	6.9	.274	-5.2	3B(123): -10.5	-0.5
2019	SFN	MLB	33	508	100	19.7	.291	0.1	3B(119): 6.6	2.6
2020	SFN	MLB	34	567	94	6.7	.291	-2.3	3B 0	0.7

Evan Longoria, continued

Batted Ball Distribution

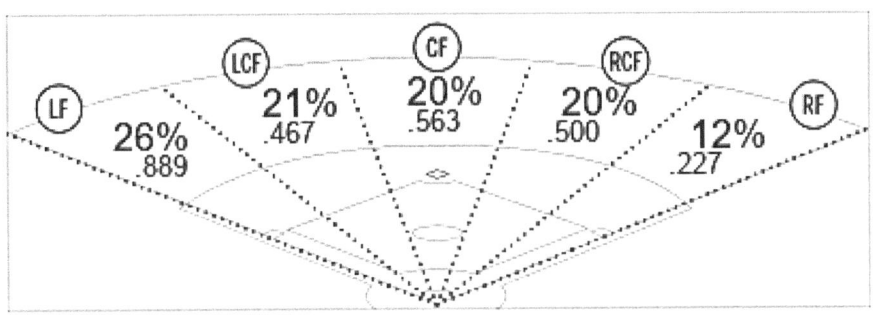

Strike Zone vs LHP   Strike Zone vs RHP

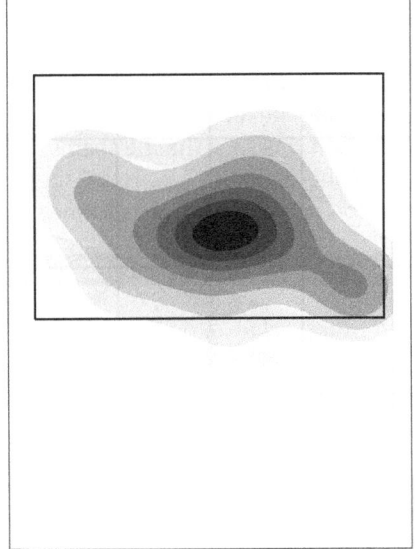

San Francisco Giants 2020

Hunter Pence OF

Born: 04/13/83   Age: 37   Bats: R   Throws: R
Height: 6'4"   Weight: 230   Origin: Round 2, 2004 Draft (#64 overall)

YEAR	TEAM	LVL	AGE	PA	R	2B	3B	HR	RBI	BB	K	SB	CS	AVG/OBP/SLG
2017	SFN	MLB	34	539	55	13	5	13	67	40	102	2	3	.260/.315/.385
2018	SAC	AAA	35	111	11	4	0	1	13	6	24	0	0	.301/.342/.369
2018	SFN	MLB	35	248	19	11	1	4	24	11	59	5	1	.226/.258/.332
2019	TEX	MLB	36	316	53	17	1	18	59	26	69	6	1	.297/.358/.552
2020	TEX	MLB	37	251	29	12	1	10	33	18	60	2	1	.261/.317/.444

Comparables: Jermaine Dye, Kendrys Morales, Glenallen Hill

The Rangers have employed some of the most beloved players in the game over the last few years: Adrián Beltré, Bartolo Colón, Tim Lincecum and now Hunter Pence. Pence spent the 2018-19 offseason revamping his swing, even going so far as to play in the Dominican Winter League to get the new swing a little in-game action. He signed a minor-league deal with his hometown Rangers and proceeded to make the Opening Day roster. To the untrained eye, the new swing still looked like a Tasmanian Devil trying to kill an aggressive pterodactyl, but the results didn't lie: by July, Pence had made one more roster, as he was named to his fourth career All-Star team. Injuries beset the veteran in the second half—he didn't play after August 22 due to a lower back injury—but his production was such that he seems likely to get another shot somewhere in 2020. If not (or if it's not Texas), Ranger fans were fortunate to get one season to cheer for one of the game's all-time good dudes.

YEAR	TEAM	LVL	AGE	PA	DRC+	VORP	BABIP	BRR	FRAA	WARP
2017	SFN	MLB	34	539	89	16.4	.301	4.4	RF(125): 2.0	1.1
2018	SAC	AAA	35	111	96	1.9	.380	-0.1	RF(12): 0.1, LF(11): 0.2	0.2
2018	SFN	MLB	35	248	66	-2.6	.282	0.4	LF(44): -3.1, RF(12): -1.2	-0.8
2019	TEX	MLB	36	316	122	15.3	.333	0.9	LF(16): 1.1, RF(8): 0.1	1.7
2020	TEX	MLB	37	251	101	9.4	.314	1.0	RF 1, LF 1	1.1

Hunter Pence, continued

Batted Ball Distribution

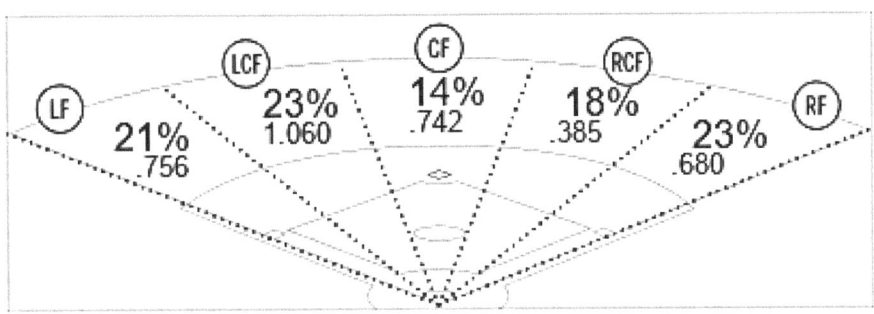

Strike Zone vs LHP **Strike Zone vs RHP**

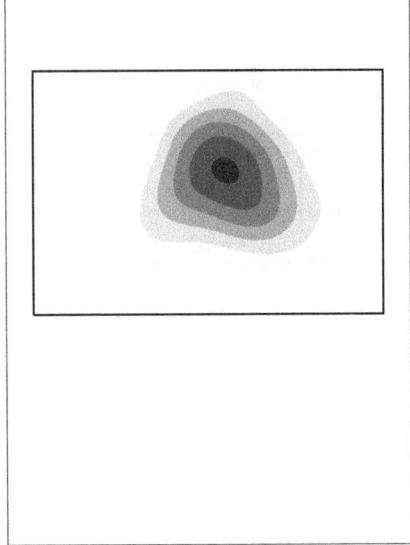

San Francisco Giants 2020

Buster Posey C

Born: 03/27/87   Age: 33   Bats: R   Throws: R
Height: 6'1"   Weight: 210   Origin: Round 1, 2008 Draft (#5 overall)

YEAR	TEAM	LVL	AGE	PA	R	2B	3B	HR	RBI	BB	K	SB	CS	AVG/OBP/SLG
2017	SFN	MLB	30	568	62	34	0	12	67	61	66	6	1	.320/.400/.462
2018	SFN	MLB	31	448	47	22	1	5	41	45	53	3	2	.284/.359/.382
2019	SFN	MLB	32	445	43	24	0	7	38	34	71	0	0	.257/.320/.368
2020	SFN	MLB	33	497	50	24	1	9	50	45	77	3	1	.263/.335/.380

Comparables: Earl Battey, Ramon Hernandez, Mike Piazza

YEAR	TEAM	P. COUNT	FRM RUNS	BLK RUNS	THRW RUNS	TOT RUNS
2017	SFN	13474	4.8	0.2	2.3	7.4
2018	SFN	12224	0.9	0.7	0.1	2.0
2019	SFN	13869	10.1	2.2	1.6	13.8
2020	SFN	19239	10.0	1.1	1.3	12.3

Unquestionably the most valuable Giants player of the decade, there's a great argument that Posey is the decade's signature player. After all, not only does he have three World Series rings with the decade's only true dynasty, but his position has been the center of a revolution in sabermetrics. (Posey himself is, undoubtedly, one of the greatest in the game at framing pitches for extra strikes.) He entered the league at an early age, one of the vanguards of the game's recent youth movement, where pre-free agency players have been providing more value than ever before as compared to their veteran counterparts. With the decade now complete, its signature player is one of those less-productive veterans, and hip surgery—*could there be a more old-player injury?*—appears to have robbed him of much of his offensive swagger. There's no chance he can be as great as he was during his prime, but now the Giants legend will look to stay behind the plate as long as he can, providing defensive value and leadership while looking to regain his stroke.

YEAR	TEAM	LVL	AGE	PA	DRC+	VORP	BABIP	BRR	FRAA	WARP
2017	SFN	MLB	30	568	129	49.2	.347	-1.5	C(99): 7.0, 1B(38): 3.5	5.2
2018	SFN	MLB	31	448	107	20.6	.316	-1.3	C(88): 0.1, 1B(13): 1.5	2.4
2019	SFN	MLB	32	445	86	14.4	.296	-1.4	C(101): 14.9, 1B(4): -0.1	2.7
2020	SFN	MLB	33	497	93	15.9	.300	-1.2	C 12, 1B 2	3.2

Buster Posey, continued

Batted Ball Distribution

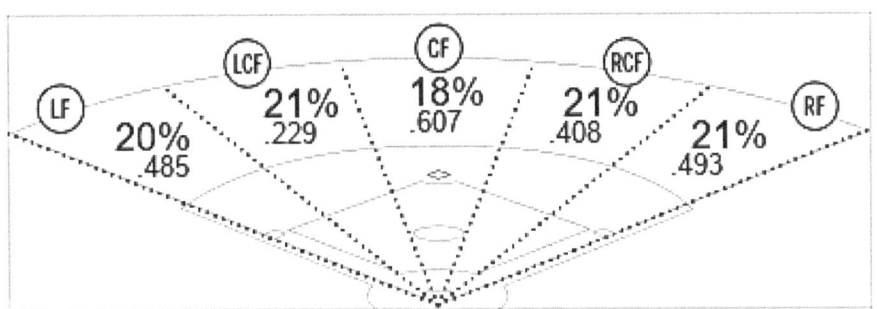

Strike Zone vs LHP

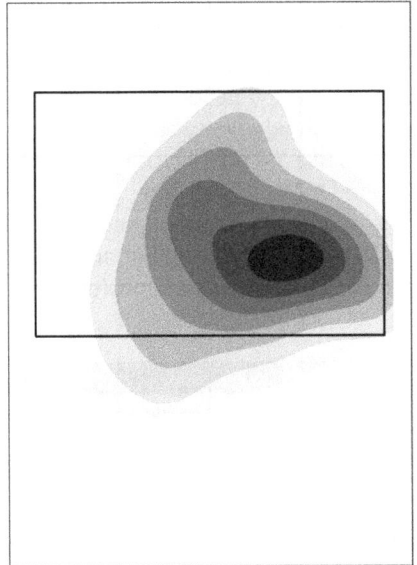

Strike Zone vs RHP

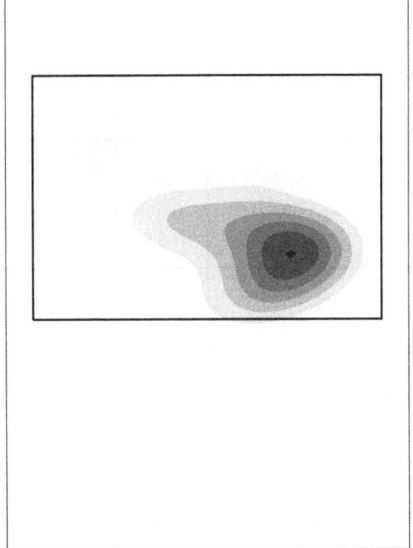

San Francisco Giants 2020

Joey Rickard OF

Born: 05/21/91 Age: 29 Bats: R Throws: L
Height: 6'1" Weight: 185 Origin: Round 9, 2012 Draft (#302 overall)

YEAR	TEAM	LVL	AGE	PA	R	2B	3B	HR	RBI	BB	K	SB	CS	AVG/OBP/SLG
2017	NOR	AAA	26	58	8	1	0	1	4	11	9	0	0	.191/.345/.277
2017	BAL	MLB	26	277	29	15	0	4	19	9	63	8	1	.241/.276/.345
2018	NOR	AAA	27	185	25	13	1	2	27	26	28	3	0	.275/.384/.412
2018	BAL	MLB	27	230	27	10	1	8	23	15	55	4	2	.244/.300/.413
2019	SAC	AAA	28	195	45	15	2	6	23	18	27	0	2	.372/.431/.587
2019	NOR	AAA	28	77	10	5	0	4	10	11	16	1	0	.203/.338/.469
2019	BAL	MLB	28	135	10	7	2	2	6	14	33	3	2	.203/.304/.347
2019	SFN	MLB	28	54	4	2	0	1	4	4	17	1	0	.280/.333/.380
2020	SFN	MLB	29	251	24	10	1	5	24	21	61	5	2	.227/.302/.347

Comparables: David Dellucci, Bob Borkowski, Pat Sheridan

Can you believe the things this guy can do? He is a superlative athlete, easily able to accelerate and run faster than most of the humans on this planet. His hand-eye coordination is marvelous, allowing him to make consistent hard contact on his swings off diving pitches moving upwards of 95 miles per hour. He's got the reflexes and cognitive abilities to excel as a defender, even as he tracks slicing liners off the bat and corrals them with relative ease. And when it comes to his 2020 outlook, the words we have to use are pernicious things like "fringy," "below-average," and "got non-tendered by the Giants after getting waived by the Orioles." Rickard's a top athlete in one of the hardest sports leagues in the world, and still he'll need a lucky break to make a 25-man roster as a platoon option and a defensive replacement. That's how hard professional baseball is.

YEAR	TEAM	LVL	AGE	PA	DRC+	VORP	BABIP	BRR	FRAA	WARP
2017	NOR	AAA	26	58	119	1.3	.216	1.2	LF(7): 0.5, RF(6): -1.0	0.3
2017	BAL	MLB	26	277	65	-3.5	.303	0.9	RF(53): 2.8, LF(43): -1.4	-0.3
2018	NOR	AAA	27	185	139	14.5	.317	-0.1	CF(32): 4.0, LF(8): 0.4	1.7
2018	BAL	MLB	27	230	92	1.3	.293	-0.4	RF(40): 3.8, LF(36): -1.4	0.6
2019	SAC	AAA	28	195	131	18.8	.408	2.1	LF(26): 0.0, CF(10): 0.3	1.4
2019	NOR	AAA	28	77	107	2.6	.205	0.2	LF(8): 1.9, RF(5): 1.1	0.5
2019	BAL	MLB	28	135	76	-0.2	.265	0.5	RF(23): -1.6, CF(16): -0.2	-0.1
2019	SFN	MLB	28	54	60	-1.3	.406	0.7	LF(20): 0.0, RF(2): -0.1	-0.1
2020	SFN	MLB	29	251	76	0.7	.290	0.3	LF 0, RF 1	0.3

Joey Rickard, continued

Batted Ball Distribution

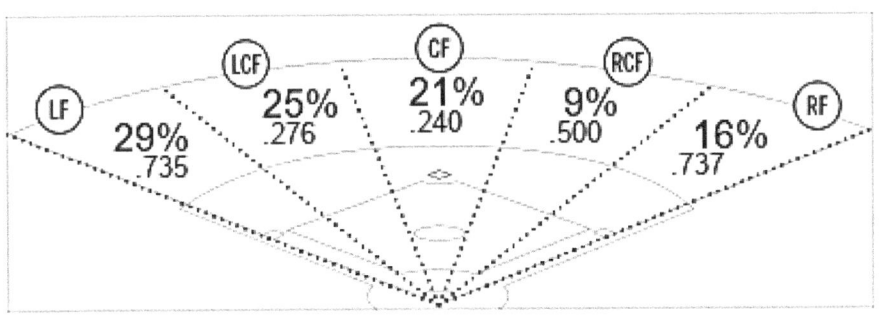

Strike Zone vs LHP   **Strike Zone vs RHP**

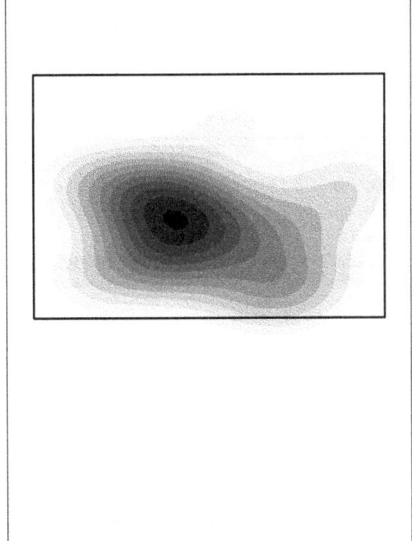

Pablo Sandoval 3B

Born: 08/11/86 Age: 33 Bats: B Throws: R
Height: 5'11" Weight: 268 Origin: International Free Agent, 2003

YEAR	TEAM	LVL	AGE	PA	R	2B	3B	HR	RBI	BB	K	SB	CS	AVG/OBP/SLG
2017	PAW	AAA	30	81	7	3	0	1	4	4	16	0	0	.221/.259/.299
2017	SAC	AAA	30	37	4	1	0	1	3	5	3	0	0	.207/.324/.345
2017	BOS	MLB	30	108	10	2	0	4	12	8	24	0	1	.212/.269/.354
2017	SFN	MLB	30	171	17	9	0	5	20	8	29	0	0	.225/.263/.375
2018	SFN	MLB	31	252	22	10	1	9	40	19	52	0	0	.248/.310/.417
2019	SFN	MLB	32	296	42	23	0	14	41	18	67	1	0	.268/.313/.507
2020	SFN	MLB	33	251	25	11	0	9	30	16	55	0	0	.223/.279/.386

Comparables: Adrián Beltré, Ryan Zimmerman, Mike Moustakas

Against long odds, the man they call Panda had his first above-replacement season since his previous Giants run, only this year didn't end with a parade. Instead of a fixture at a single position, he's now more of an instant-offense corner infield reserve, a switch-hitter especially effective against lefties but a liability in the field. Free agency should be … interesting for him, where he's likely to get something more like a minor-league invite than the nine-figure deal he wrapped the last time around. Although he's only going into his age-34 season, his (in)famous stature and conditioning, a late-season elbow surgery, and how downright terrible he was anywhere other than San Francisco might make teams hesitant to offer him anything more than a token contract to be a highly likable bench bat.

YEAR	TEAM	LVL	AGE	PA	DRC+	VORP	BABIP	BRR	FRAA	WARP
2017	PAW	AAA	30	81	68	-2.9	.267	-0.5	3B(15): -1.6	-0.2
2017	SAC	AAA	30	37	81	1.4	.185	-0.1	3B(7): 1.2	0.1
2017	BOS	MLB	30	108	81	-1.8	.236	-0.2	3B(29): -1.4, 2B(1): 0.0	0.0
2017	SFN	MLB	30	171	80	-1.0	.242	-0.4	3B(38): -2.6, 1B(9): -0.1	-0.2
2018	SFN	MLB	31	252	96	1.6	.282	-2.8	3B(36): -1.8, 1B(24): -1.4	-0.1
2019	SFN	MLB	32	296	98	8.5	.304	0.0	3B(45): -4.1, 1B(23): 0.1	0.4
2020	SFN	MLB	33	251	74	-0.9	.256	-0.7	3B -4, 1B 0	-0.5

Pablo Sandoval, continued

Batted Ball Distribution

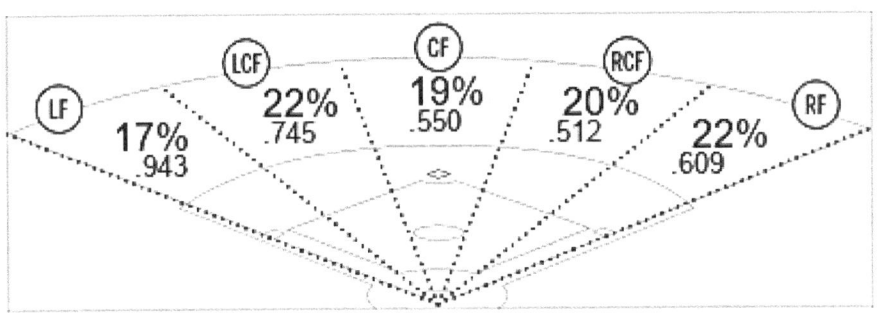

Strike Zone vs LHP

Strike Zone vs RHP

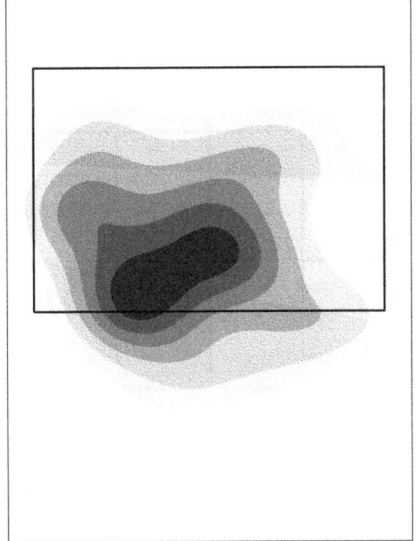

San Francisco Giants 2020

Austin Slater UT

Born: 12/13/92   Age: 27   Bats: R   Throws: R
Height: 6'2"   Weight: 197   Origin: Round 8, 2014 Draft (#238 overall)

YEAR	TEAM	LVL	AGE	PA	R	2B	3B	HR	RBI	BB	K	SB	CS	AVG/OBP/SLG
2017	SAC	AAA	24	206	28	12	0	5	27	15	39	4	3	.321/.377/.467
2017	SFN	MLB	24	127	15	3	1	3	16	8	29	0	0	.282/.339/.402
2018	SAC	AAA	25	223	32	24	2	5	32	21	39	8	2	.344/.417/.564
2018	SFN	MLB	25	225	21	6	1	1	23	20	69	7	0	.251/.333/.307
2019	SAC	AAA	26	296	47	17	0	12	45	46	69	6	2	.308/.436/.529
2019	SFN	MLB	26	192	20	9	3	5	21	22	59	1	0	.238/.333/.417
2020	SFN	MLB	27	413	44	16	1	10	44	42	120	5	2	.242/.329/.376

Comparables: Dick Williams, Junior Lake, Joe Adcock

Slater, a Jacksonville native who has spent his college and pro careers playing mostly in California, has picked up a trick or two since exiting Duval County. There's his opposite-field approach, adopted at Stanford and honed in the upper minors; this has caused him to wreak havoc on Triple-A pitching but hasn't yet translated into sustained big-league success. There's the collection of gloves he's picked up while trying out new positions; while best suited for the corners, he handled nearly every spot on the diamond last year and best profiles as a sort of super-utility hand. And then there's the advice from Barry Bonds that may have led to a dynamite August run for the big club: *only swing at pitches you can drive*. With everything he's learned along the way, a spot appears open for him as the soft side of a roving platoon, able to beat up lefties while spelling players all over the field.

YEAR	TEAM	LVL	AGE	PA	DRC+	VORP	BABIP	BRR	FRAA	WARP
2017	SAC	AAA	24	206	116	9.5	.380	-2.7	RF(22): -0.9, LF(17): -0.1	0.7
2017	SFN	MLB	24	127	84	4.6	.353	0.2	LF(30): -1.0, RF(3): -0.2	0.0
2018	SAC	AAA	25	223	159	22.2	.405	1.4	RF(29): 0.6, 1B(13): -0.1	2.1
2018	SFN	MLB	25	225	64	1.9	.377	1.3	LF(25): 1.8, 1B(21): 0.1	-0.2
2019	SAC	AAA	26	296	139	30.0	.388	0.6	1B(38): 2.5, 3B(11): -1.4	2.1
2019	SFN	MLB	26	192	73	-2.0	.337	-0.7	RF(46): -0.2, 1B(8): -0.8	-0.4
2020	SFN	MLB	27	413	93	6.5	.332	-0.3	RF -1, LF 0	0.6

Austin Slater, continued

Batted Ball Distribution

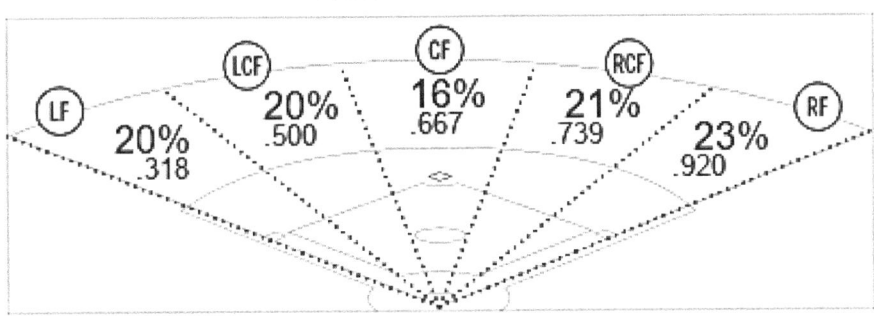

Strike Zone vs LHP Strike Zone vs RHP

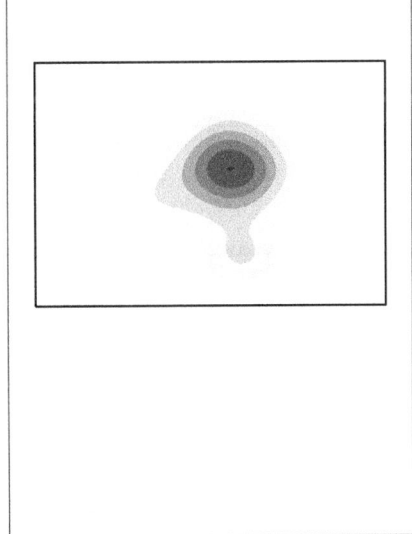

Giants Player Analysis - 49

Donovan Solano INF

Born: 12/17/87 Age: 32 Bats: R Throws: R
Height: 5'10" Weight: 205 Origin: International Free Agent, 2005

YEAR	TEAM	LVL	AGE	PA	R	2B	3B	HR	RBI	BB	K	SB	CS	AVG/OBP/SLG
2017	SWB	AAA	29	405	44	29	0	4	48	24	60	1	0	.282/.329/.391
2018	DOD	RK	30	27	3	1	0	0	3	0	1	0	0	.440/.444/.480
2018	OKL	AAA	30	340	38	21	1	4	43	16	40	4	1	.318/.353/.430
2019	SAC	AAA	31	97	12	4	0	2	16	9	11	0	0	.322/.392/.437
2019	SFN	MLB	31	228	27	13	1	4	23	10	49	0	1	.330/.360/.456
2020	SFN	MLB	32	315	28	15	1	5	30	15	66	1	0	.268/.310/.371

Comparables: Adam Kennedy, Emilio Bonifácio, Orlando Hudson

If you predicted Solano would be the most productive regular in the Giants' middle infield this year, we're checking your garage for a souped-up DeLorean. Never an exceptional defender or even an average hitter, the veteran utility man spent most of the past three seasons propping up the infields for various Triple-A squads since his few years as a regular on disappointing Marlins teams. A desperate San Francisco squad turned to the Colombian in May, and he finally showed out at the plate in the bigs during his age-31 season. There's reason to think that the surprising .330 batting average is a bit of a fluke, and that his flurry of doubles is more indicative of a jacked-up ball than a change in his skill level. But whether Solano returns to the upper minors or sticks around as a big-league bench piece, he's re-established himself as a reliable depth option with the potential to drop in a choice base hit.

YEAR	TEAM	LVL	AGE	PA	DRC+	VORP	BABIP	BRR	FRAA	WARP
2017	SWB	AAA	29	405	108	6.2	.324	-0.8	2B(59): 2.3, 3B(28): 2.4	1.9
2018	DOD	RK	30	27	189	3.6	.440	-0.1	SS(5): 1.6, 2B(1): 0.0	0.5
2018	OKL	AAA	30	340	108	20.9	.348	-1.2	SS(65): -1.9, 2B(10): 0.7	1.6
2019	SAC	AAA	31	97	112	4.1	.351	-0.9	2B(14): 0.4, 3B(10): 0.3	0.5
2019	SFN	MLB	31	228	101	9.0	.409	1.7	2B(36): -2.6, SS(19): 0.5	0.9
2020	SFN	MLB	32	315	83	6.3	.331	1.3	2B 0, SS 0	0.7

Donovan Solano, continued

Batted Ball Distribution

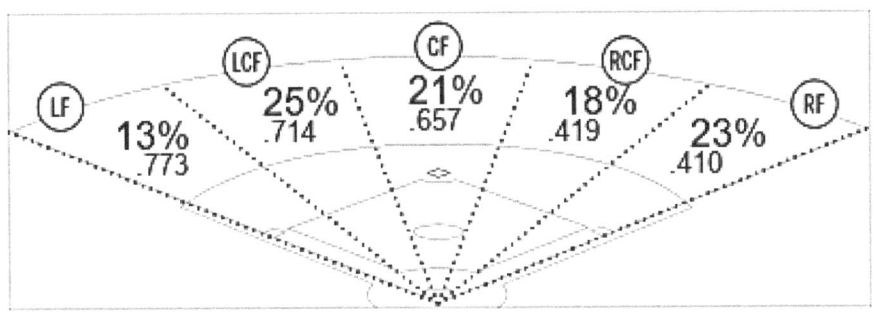

Strike Zone vs LHP   Strike Zone vs RHP

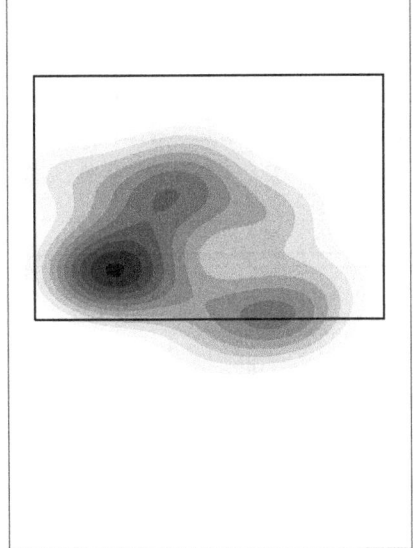

Yolmer Sánchez 2B

Born: 06/29/92 Age: 28 Bats: B Throws: R
Height: 5'11" Weight: 185 Origin: International Free Agent, 2009

YEAR	TEAM	LVL	AGE	PA	R	2B	3B	HR	RBI	BB	K	SB	CS	AVG/OBP/SLG
2017	CHA	MLB	25	534	63	19	8	12	59	35	111	8	9	.267/.319/.413
2018	CHA	MLB	26	662	62	34	10	8	55	49	138	14	6	.242/.306/.372
2019	CHA	MLB	27	555	59	20	4	2	43	44	117	5	4	.252/.318/.321
2020	CHA	MLB	28	251	23	10	2	5	24	17	54	4	2	.235/.295/.352

Comparables: Asdrúbal Cabrera, Rubén Tejada, Bret Boone

The balls were pretty juicy back in 2017, when Sánchez's stilted uncoil of a swing produced a career-high 12 home runs and he flirted with league-average offensive production. Two years later, they were even juicier, and…he posted the lowest ISO of any qualified hitter in the game. Hmph. To his credit, he's leaned in hard to both sides of his light-hitting, nimble glove profile over the last three years—his Gold Glove win was legitimate, in our estimation. All jokes are funnier when you're hitting 20 bombs per year, which is a shame because Sánchez ambushing random teammates and coaches who aren't looking with Gatorade baths during walk-off dogpiles is one of baseball's best running bits.

YEAR	TEAM	LVL	AGE	PA	DRC+	VORP	BABIP	BRR	FRAA	WARP
2017	CHA	MLB	25	534	93	13.8	.321	0.9	2B(78): -0.3, 3B(52): 3.2	1.6
2018	CHA	MLB	26	662	80	11.4	.300	0.7	3B(141): -1.2, 2B(9): 0.2	0.7
2019	CHA	MLB	27	555	78	2.3	.324	0.2	2B(149): 19.0	2.1
2020	CHA	MLB	28	251	75	0.3	.289	0.4	2B 2, 3B 1	0.3

Yolmer Sánchez, continued

Batted Ball Distribution

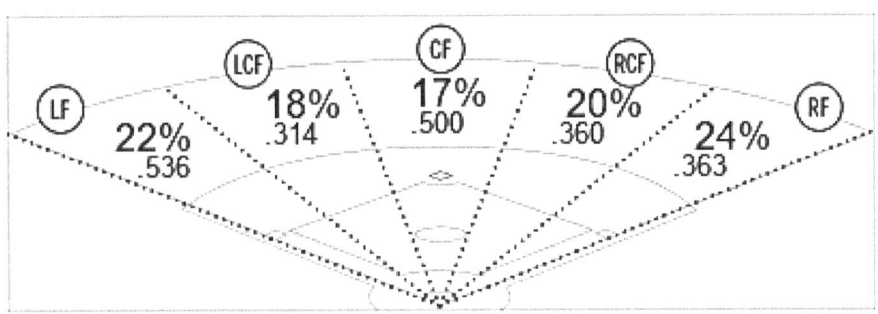

Strike Zone vs LHP   Strike Zone vs RHP

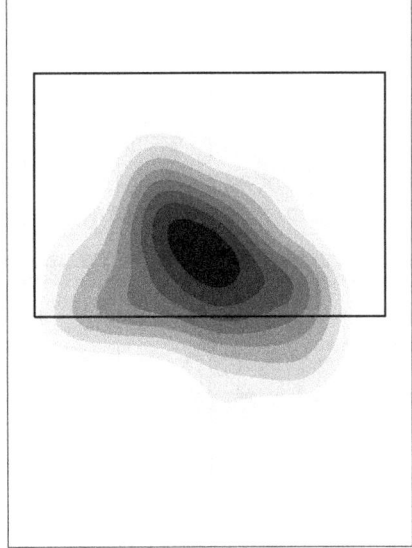

San Francisco Giants 2020

Mike Yastrzemski   LF
Born: 08/23/90   Age: 29   Bats: L   Throws: L
Height: 5'11"   Weight: 180   Origin: Round 14, 2013 Draft (#429 overall)

YEAR	TEAM	LVL	AGE	PA	R	2B	3B	HR	RBI	BB	K	SB	CS	AVG/OBP/SLG
2017	BOW	AA	26	94	20	6	1	6	19	9	17	1	1	.386/.436/.699
2017	NOR	AAA	26	307	41	15	3	9	41	31	74	2	1	.240/.322/.417
2018	BOW	AA	27	117	13	10	0	1	11	10	30	2	1	.202/.276/.327
2018	NOR	AAA	27	374	48	18	6	9	49	44	75	6	4	.265/.359/.441
2019	SAC	AAA	28	163	38	11	1	12	25	22	36	2	2	.316/.414/.676
2019	SFN	MLB	28	411	64	22	3	21	55	32	107	2	4	.272/.334/.518
2020	SFN	MLB	29	504	56	21	3	19	63	43	138	5	2	.230/.303/.416

Comparables: George Shuba, John Andreoli, Brian Goodwin

Proof that even mid-season "organizational depth" trades can sometimes change everything, Yaz the Younger was the most visible bright spot for the 2019 Giants. Prior to this season, he was considered an upper-minors depth piece, an outfielder without the standout skills to hold down a regular job in the majors. But as a 28-year-old rookie, the Giants gave him the opportunity to play and he ran with it, displaying surprising newfound power and getting just a bit lucky with his batting average on balls in play. That power was on display during what might've been the signature moment of the 2019 Giants' season: On the road in Boston in September, Yaz III hung out with his grandfather before the game, patrolled grandad's old spot in left field during it, and then took Nate Eovaldi deep to help give the Giants their first win at Fenway in literally a century.

YEAR	TEAM	LVL	AGE	PA	DRC+	VORP	BABIP	BRR	FRAA	WARP
2017	BOW	AA	26	94	183	13.8	.419	-0.5	RF(12): -0.3, CF(4): -0.2	0.9
2017	NOR	AAA	26	307	109	11.3	.295	1.8	LF(36): 3.1, RF(30): 3.6	1.9
2018	BOW	AA	27	117	75	1.2	.270	1.5	LF(14): 0.9, RF(7): 1.5	0.4
2018	NOR	AAA	27	374	134	25.7	.320	4.3	LF(50): 8.7, CF(36): 2.2	4.0
2019	SAC	AAA	28	163	145	23.7	.344	2.2	CF(21): -0.2, LF(8): -0.3	1.6
2019	SFN	MLB	28	411	112	17.0	.325	0.5	LF(61): -0.5, RF(56): 0.3	1.7
2020	SFN	MLB	29	504	93	11.1	.287	1.1	RF 6, CF 1	1.8

Mike Yastrzemski, continued

Batted Ball Distribution

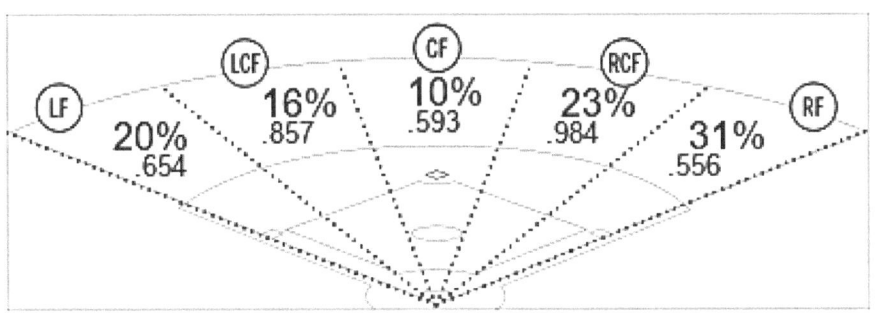

Strike Zone vs LHP   **Strike Zone vs RHP**

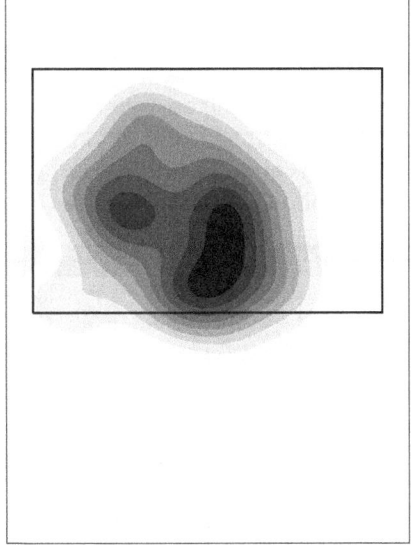

San Francisco Giants 2020

Shaun Anderson   RHP

Born: 10/29/94   Age: 25   Bats: R   Throws: R
Height: 6'4"   Weight: 225   Origin: Round 3, 2016 Draft (#88 overall)

YEAR	TEAM	LVL	AGE	W	L	SV	G	GS	IP	H	HR	BB/9	K/9	K	GB%	BABIP
2017	GRN	A	22	3	0	0	7	7	38^2	30	2	2.6	8.6	37	52%	.272
2017	SLM	A+	22	3	3	0	11	11	58^2	53	6	2.8	7.4	48	43%	.270
2017	SJO	A+	22	3	3	0	6	5	25^2	19	1	1.4	7.7	22	51%	.247
2018	RIC	AA	23	6	5	0	17	16	94	93	9	2.1	8.9	93	49%	.316
2018	SAC	AAA	23	2	2	0	8	8	47^1	48	5	2.1	6.5	34	47%	.287
2019	SAC	AAA	24	2	1	0	8	8	38^1	36	3	3.1	9.6	41	54%	.317
2019	SFN	MLB	24	3	5	2	28	16	96	111	13	3.6	6.6	70	43%	.322
2020	SFN	MLB	25	2	3	17	50	0	53	57	7	3.3	6.7	40	44%	.301

Comparables: Justin Grimm, Cody Martin, Aaron Blair

A slider that gets missed 30 percent of the time it's swung at … that's a good pitch. You'd think with a pitch like that, Anderson might've gotten a few more strikeouts during his debut season. But instead of taking the league by storm, the former Gator had trouble putting hitters away, whether he was starting or ending games … it was pretty much a litany of troubles. After dropping out of the rotation, he got a crack at the closer job, but his first-inning struggles as a starter translated all too well to the first innings of his relief work too. After three years of posting solid numbers in the minors, the shock of struggles at the big-league level could have been a surprise, but there's still enough of a foundation to expect him to grow into a role as a back-end starter or late-inning reliever.

YEAR	TEAM	LVL	AGE	WHIP	ERA	DRA	WARP	MPH	FB%	WHF	CSP
2017	GRN	A	22	1.06	2.56	3.65	0.7				
2017	SLM	A+	22	1.21	3.99	3.88	0.9				
2017	SJO	A+	22	0.90	3.51	2.64	0.8				
2018	RIC	AA	23	1.22	3.45	4.21	1.2				
2018	SAC	AAA	23	1.25	4.18	4.11	0.8				
2019	SAC	AAA	24	1.28	3.76	2.92	1.4				
2019	SFN	MLB	24	1.55	5.44	6.51	-0.8	95.1	58.5	10	46.4
2020	SFN	MLB	25	1.44	4.46	5.00	0.3	94.8	59.9	10.3	47.5

Shaun Anderson, continued

Pitch Shape vs LHH

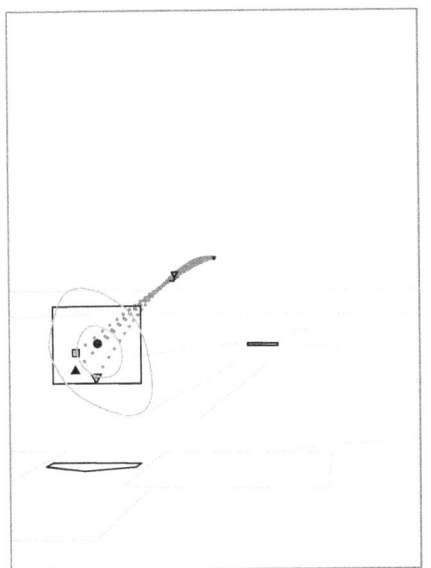

Pitch Shape vs RHH

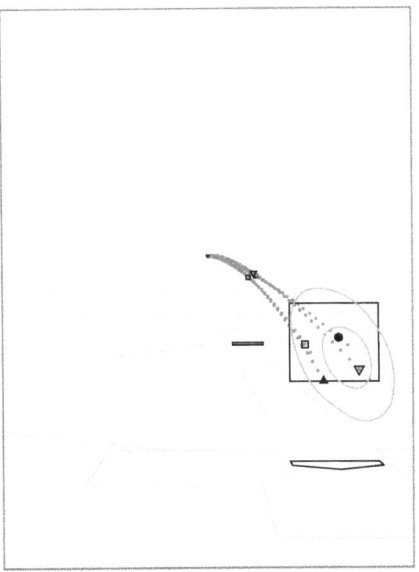

Type	Frequency	Velocity	H Movement	V Movement
● Fastball	45.1%	92.9 [101]	0.2 [131]	-15.7 [101]
☐ Sinker	13.4%	92.8 [101]	-8.6 [126]	-17.6 [110]
+ Cutter				
▲ Changeup	8.3%	86.3 [104]	-7.7 [116]	-26.4 [103]
✕ Splitter				
▽ Slider	29.9%	86.7 [110]	5.6 [102]	-31.4 [105]
◇ Curveball	3.3%	78.5 [100]	5.8 [93]	-49.7 [95]
⊕ Slow Curveball				
✳ Knuckleball				
▼ Screwball				

Tyler Anderson LHP

Born: 12/30/89 Age: 30 Bats: L Throws: L
Height: 6'3" Weight: 215 Origin: Round 1, 2011 Draft (#20 overall)

YEAR	TEAM	LVL	AGE	W	L	SV	G	GS	IP	H	HR	BB/9	K/9	K	GB%	BABIP
2017	ABQ	AAA	27	0	2	0	4	2	12^1	14	0	2.9	9.5	13	35%	.412
2017	COL	MLB	27	6	6	0	17	15	86	88	16	2.7	8.5	81	46%	.304
2018	COL	MLB	28	7	9	0	32	32	176	165	30	3.0	8.4	164	38%	.281
2019	COL	MLB	29	0	3	0	5	5	20^2	33	8	4.8	10.0	23	42%	.391
2020	SFN	MLB	30	7	8	0	23	23	122	113	20	3.1	8.1	111	40%	.275

Comparables: Sam Gaviglio, Josh Outman, Steven Matz

Years of knee pain culminated in season-ending surgery in June for Anderson. The recovery period is almost as significant as the length of time that the former first-round pick has been suffering with the issue (a chondral defect in his left knee) with Anderson unlikely to be ready to begin the 2020 season. In hindsight, it's remarkable that the left-hander was able to make 32 starts the season prior. The extent to which the knee affected his performance may not become clear until, or if, he returns to full health. While the injury led Colorado to non-tender him, it does mean Anderson has the opportunity to get back on track in a rather more forgiving environment.

YEAR	TEAM	LVL	AGE	WHIP	ERA	DRA	WARP	MPH	FB%	WHF	CSP
2017	ABQ	AAA	27	1.46	4.38	4.12	0.2				
2017	COL	MLB	27	1.33	4.81	4.15	1.3	94.5	47.1	12.4	47.6
2018	COL	MLB	28	1.27	4.55	4.82	1.0	94.1	44.6	12.3	50
2019	COL	MLB	29	2.13	11.76	5.69	0.0	93.2	47.6	12.3	50
2020	SFN	MLB	30	1.26	3.70	4.42	1.9	93.4	45.4	12.3	49.2

Tyler Anderson, continued

Pitch Shape vs LHH

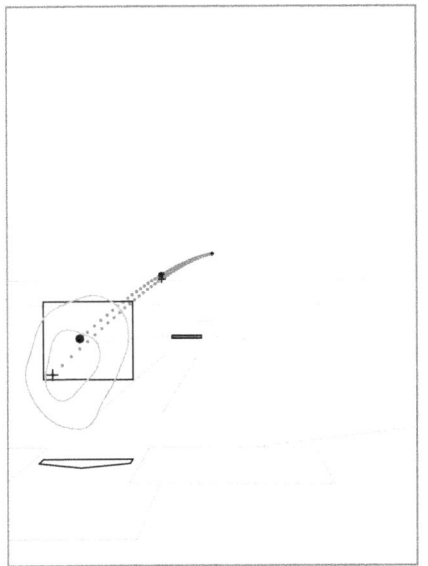

Pitch Shape vs RHH

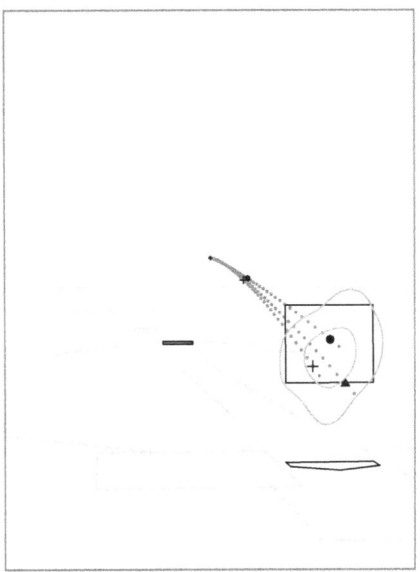

Type	Frequency	Velocity	H Movement	V Movement
● Fastball	44.1%	91.4 [97]	7.3 [98]	-13 [108]
☐ Sinker	3.5%	91.1 [92]	12 [104]	-16.7 [113]
+ Cutter	20.0%	87.1 [90]	-1.1 [95]	-20.8 [112]
▲ Changeup	25.9%	80.1 [81]	10.1 [105]	-25.7 [105]
✕ Splitter				
▽ Slider				
◇ Curveball	6.4%	73.6 [84]	-1.1 [74]	-52.6 [89]
⊕ Slow Curveball				
✳ Knuckleball				
▼ Screwball				

Giants Player Analysis - 59

San Francisco Giants 2020

Tyler Beede RHP

Born: 05/23/93 Age: 27 Bats: R Throws: R
Height: 6'3" Weight: 211 Origin: Round 1, 2014 Draft (#14 overall)

YEAR	TEAM	LVL	AGE	W	L	SV	G	GS	IP	H	HR	BB/9	K/9	K	GB%	BABIP
2017	SAC	AAA	24	6	7	0	19	19	109	121	14	3.2	6.9	83	52%	.316
2018	SAC	AAA	25	4	9	0	33	10	74	82	10	6.8	9.1	75	41%	.346
2018	SFN	MLB	25	0	1	0	2	2	7^2	9	0	9.4	10.6	9	46%	.409
2019	SAC	AAA	26	2	2	0	7	7	34^2	24	3	3.6	12.7	49	35%	.296
2019	SFN	MLB	26	5	10	0	24	22	117	127	22	3.5	8.7	113	45%	.312
2020	SFN	MLB	27	6	9	0	36	19	115	120	17	4.4	9.2	117	43%	.322

Comparables: Kyle McGowin, Chris Ellis, Rookie Davis

Finally.

The Giants faithful (and their team staff) have been waiting for the former first-round draft pick to step up and be a regular part of the team's rotation. After five consecutive years on our Giants Top 10 Prospects list, Beede finally surfaced as a regular part of the starting rotation and it was … mostly okay? There were flashes of excellence amidst an overall disappointing season. His command is still an open issue, and in trying to harness it, he gave up more home runs than he could safely absorb. However, he still has the swing-and-miss stuff that made him such a fascinating (if long-lasting) prospect, and he could stand to benefit from increased use of his bender; his curveball wasn't relied on too often, but when hitters swung at it, they missed it more than half the time. So far, the Giants stand with loads of back-of-the-rotation options, but Beede may have more upside than most of his competitors. Look for him to stick around the majors for a while longer, ceding the space on prospect lists once and for all.

YEAR	TEAM	LVL	AGE	WHIP	ERA	DRA	WARP	MPH	FB%	WHF	CSP
2017	SAC	AAA	24	1.47	4.79	4.96	0.9				
2018	SAC	AAA	25	1.86	7.05	6.99	-1.3				
2018	SFN	MLB	25	2.22	8.22	4.22	0.1	95.3	51.8	11.5	41.3
2019	SAC	AAA	26	1.10	2.34	2.42	1.4				
2019	SFN	MLB	26	1.48	5.08	5.24	0.7	96.0	56.2	12	45.3
2020	SFN	MLB	27	1.53	4.89	5.23	0.7	95.5	56.6	12.2	44.1

Tyler Beede, continued

Pitch Shape vs LHH

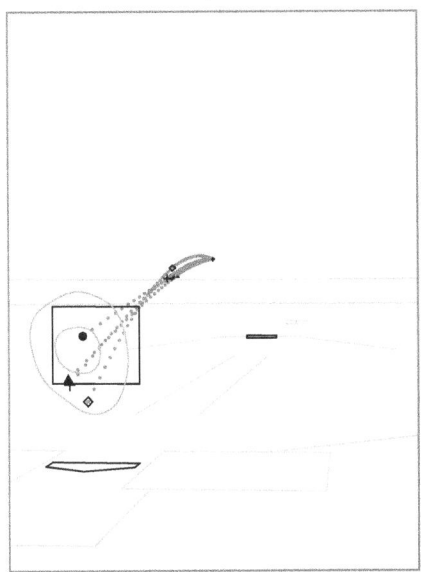

Pitch Shape vs RHH

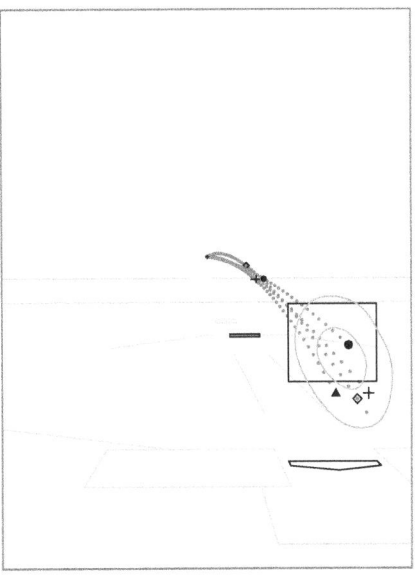

Type	Frequency	Velocity	H Movement	V Movement
● Fastball	56.2%	94.5 [106]	-8.8 [91]	-14.8 [103]
☐ Sinker				
+ Cutter	10.7%	86.4 [85]	1.8 [100]	-30.2 [77]
▲ Changeup	18.7%	84.1 [96]	-12.1 [96]	-30.7 [90]
✕ Splitter				
▽ Slider				
◇ Curveball	13.7%	80.5 [106]	7.3 [99]	-51 [93]
✦ Slow Curveball				
✱ Knuckleball				
▼ Screwball				

Sam Coonrod   RHP
Born: 09/22/92   Age: 27   Bats: R   Throws: R
Height: 6'2"   Weight: 225   Origin: Round 5, 2014 Draft (#148 overall)

YEAR	TEAM	LVL	AGE	W	L	SV	G	GS	IP	H	HR	BB/9	K/9	K	GB%	BABIP
2017	RIC	AA	24	4	11	0	24	18	103^2	96	7	3.6	8.2	94	47%	.302
2018	SJO	A+	25	0	0	0	6	0	6^1	5	0	2.8	18.5	13	33%	.417
2019	SAC	AAA	26	2	4	3	33	1	32^1	41	4	5.0	12.0	43	46%	.416
2019	SFN	MLB	26	5	1	0	33	0	27^2	19	3	4.9	6.5	20	51%	.222
2020	SFN	MLB	27	2	2	0	45	0	47	47	6	4.4	8.2	43	45%	.301

Comparables: Warwick Saupold, Ryne Stanek, Drew Gagnon

In theory, this rookie reliever has all the makings of a potential relief ace. A former starting prospect who blew out his elbow and moved to the bullpen, his return to pitching came with a bevy of strikeouts during his tour in Sacramento on the strength of his 96-mile per hour fastball and two viable secondaries. Command still seems to be an issue, both when in the minors and when promoted to San Francisco, but he survived last year on a steady diet of bad contact even when the whiffs failed him. The raw stuff is there, so a control upgrade could transform him from generic relief dude to bullpen stalwart.

YEAR	TEAM	LVL	AGE	WHIP	ERA	DRA	WARP	MPH	FB%	WHF	CSP
2017	RIC	AA	24	1.33	4.69	4.79	0.4				
2018	SJO	A+	25	1.11	5.68	2.76	0.2				
2019	SAC	AAA	26	1.82	6.96	5.78	0.1				
2019	SFN	MLB	26	1.23	3.58	4.71	0.2	98.5	65.3	10.4	47.4
2020	SFN	MLB	27	1.48	4.52	4.91	0.3	98.0	66.1	10.5	48

Sam Coonrod, continued

Pitch Shape vs LHH

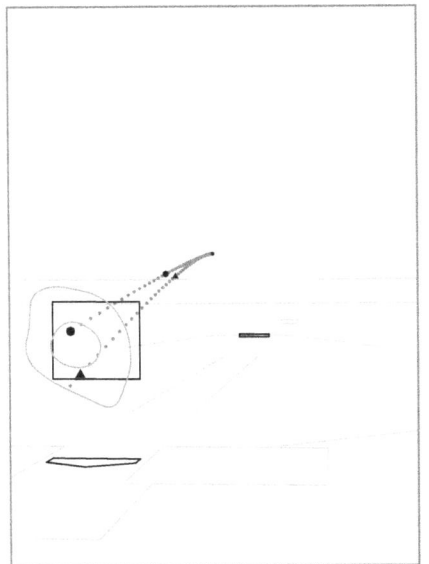

Pitch Shape vs RHH

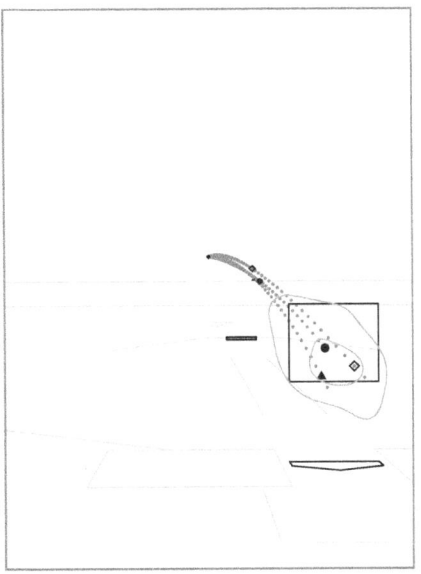

Type	Frequency	Velocity	H Movement	V Movement
● Fastball	61.9%	96.6 [112]	-11.3 [80]	-14.5 [104]
☐ Sinker	3.3%	95.7 [116]	-14.7 [87]	-17.9 [109]
+ Cutter				
▲ Changeup	17.7%	88.8 [113]	-13 [91]	-29.4 [94]
✕ Splitter				
▽ Slider				
◇ Curveball	17.0%	86.5 [126]	5.5 [92]	-37.5 [121]
⊕ Slow Curveball				
✳ Knuckleball				
▼ Screwball				

San Francisco Giants 2020

Johnny Cueto RHP
Born: 02/15/86 Age: 34 Bats: R Throws: R
Height: 5'11" Weight: 229 Origin: International Free Agent, 2004

YEAR	TEAM	LVL	AGE	W	L	SV	G	GS	IP	H	HR	BB/9	K/9	K	GB%	BABIP
2017	SJO	A+	31	0	1	0	2	2	6²	11	1	1.4	10.8	8	46%	.476
2017	SFN	MLB	31	8	8	0	25	25	147¹	160	22	3.2	8.3	136	41%	.322
2018	SAC	AAA	32	0	0	0	2	2	7²	5	0	1.2	11.7	10	39%	.278
2018	SFN	MLB	32	3	2	0	9	9	53	46	8	2.2	6.5	38	45%	.253
2019	SJO	A+	33	0	1	0	2	2	7	8	1	1.3	6.4	5	56%	.318
2019	SFN	MLB	33	1	2	0	4	4	16	11	3	5.1	7.3	13	56%	.190
2020	SFN	MLB	34	7	9	0	24	24	134	124	19	3.0	8.0	119	47%	.280

Comparables: Aníbal Sánchez, Matt Garza, Zack Greinke

Instead of keeping us waiting until 2020, Johnny Beisbol returned ahead of schedule from his Tommy John surgery rehab to make four uneven starts as a test run for 2020. Not all the signs were positive, but the best news is that his velocity is right back to where it was in 2017 and 2018 before the injury. Of course, that's a touch slower than when he was at his peak, but Cueto is tricky enough to keep batters off balance despite below-average heat. Most notable was that for the first time in a decade the veteran had trouble finding the strike zone, walking nine batters in 16 innings. Historically, command returns last after these elbow surgeries, so the Giants will be hoping that Cueto finds his soon; they'd prefer that the $43 million committed to him at least pays for a middle-of-the-rotation starter with veteran wiles.

YEAR	TEAM	LVL	AGE	WHIP	ERA	DRA	WARP	MPH	FB%	WHF	CSP
2017	SJO	A+	31	1.80	6.75	7.38	-0.2				
2017	SFN	MLB	31	1.45	4.52	4.57	1.7	93.8	51.2	11.4	42.7
2018	SAC	AAA	32	0.78	0.00	2.50	0.3				
2018	SFN	MLB	32	1.11	3.23	4.56	0.5	92.7	46.8	10	46.4
2019	SJO	A+	33	1.29	6.43	5.72	-0.1				
2019	SFN	MLB	33	1.25	5.06	4.43	0.2	92.9	51.3	7.9	42.7
2020	SFN	MLB	34	1.26	3.61	4.28	2.3	92.3	49.3	10.5	43.3

Johnny Cueto, continued

Pitch Shape vs LHH

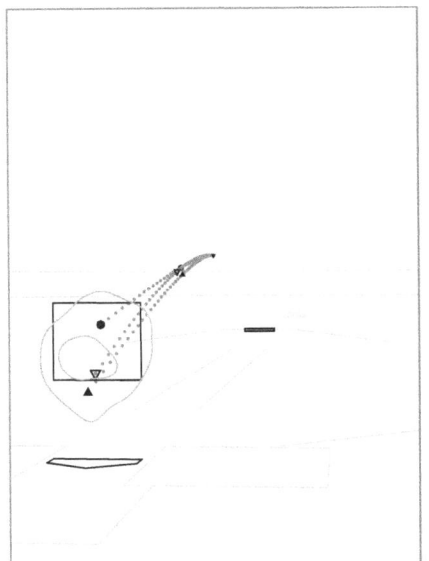

Pitch Shape vs RHH

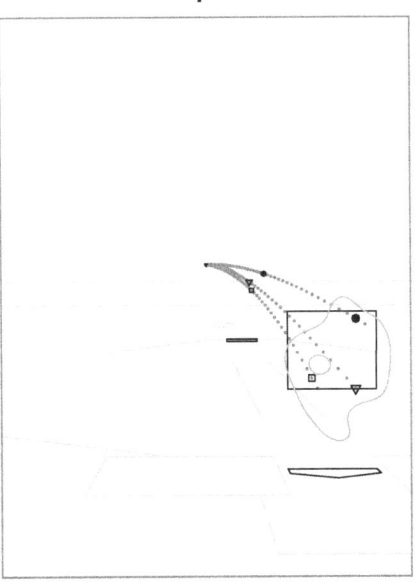

Type	Frequency	Velocity	H Movement	V Movement
● Fastball	31.7%	91.2 [97]	-7.4 [98]	-15.8 [100]
☐ Sinker	19.6%	91 [92]	-13.2 [97]	-22.3 [93]
+ Cutter				
▲ Changeup	18.5%	83.4 [93]	-8 [115]	-31.8 [87]
✕ Splitter				
▽ Slider	25.3%	84.1 [99]	2.6 [90]	-30.9 [106]
◇ Curveball	4.9%	80.6 [106]	3.7 [85]	-38.9 [118]
⊕ Slow Curveball				
✳ Knuckleball				
▼ Screwball				

Giants Player Analysis

Jarlín García LHP

Born: 01/18/93   Age: 27   Bats: L   Throws: L
Height: 6'3"   Weight: 215   Origin: International Free Agent, 2010

YEAR	TEAM	LVL	AGE	W	L	SV	G	GS	IP	H	HR	BB/9	K/9	K	GB%	BABIP
2017	MIA	MLB	24	1	2	0	68	0	53^1	47	6	2.9	7.1	42	41%	.263
2018	NWO	AAA	25	2	2	0	10	9	48^2	57	5	2.6	6.1	33	40%	.323
2018	MIA	MLB	25	3	3	0	29	7	66	59	16	3.8	5.5	40	44%	.222
2019	NWO	AAA	26	2	0	0	7	0	9^1	6	1	3.9	10.6	11	38%	.250
2019	MIA	MLB	26	4	2	0	53	0	50^2	40	4	2.8	6.9	39	48%	.248
2020	MIA	MLB	27	3	3	8	54	0	58	59	10	3.0	7.0	45	44%	.287

Comparables: Robbie Ross Jr., T.J. McFarland, Luis Cessa

García righted the ship in 2019 following an acutely disappointing sophomore effort, gaining velocity throughout the year and limiting the walks and homers that previously plagued him so. His unusually heavy four-seamer still didn't miss many bats, but García's ground-ball-oriented arsenal played up in the age of the gopher ball. Yet it was García's commitment to altering his pitch mix between righties and lefties combined with improved movement on both his fastball and slider that propelled him into high-leverage situations. Against righties, he deployed a much more democratic approach across all counts; against lefties, he almost stopped throwing his changeup altogether and instead went heavy on the slider. It's difficult to be a lefty reliever who relies on contact more than strikeouts, but García has found a path to success for now.

YEAR	TEAM	LVL	AGE	WHIP	ERA	DRA	WARP	MPH	FB%	WHF	CSP
2017	MIA	MLB	24	1.20	4.72	4.42	0.4	96.1	49.8	12.1	47.8
2018	NWO	AAA	25	1.46	4.81	5.41	0.1				
2018	MIA	MLB	25	1.32	4.91	5.51	-0.3	94.2	52.5	8.4	49.3
2019	NWO	AAA	26	1.07	1.93	3.35	0.3				
2019	MIA	MLB	26	1.11	3.02	3.92	0.8	95.1	39.8	9.8	51.8
2020	MIA	MLB	27	1.36	4.52	4.77	0.4	94.5	47.9	10	50.6

Jarlin García, continued

Pitch Shape vs LHH

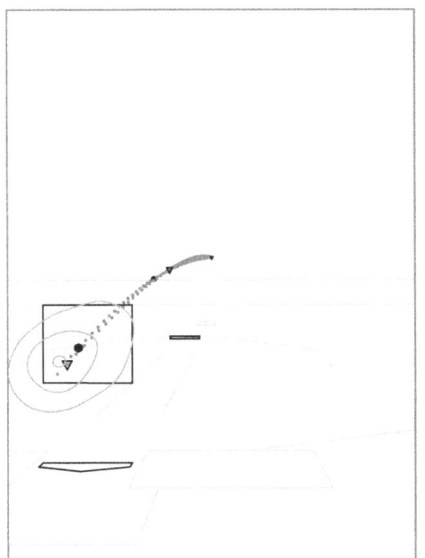

Pitch Shape vs RHH

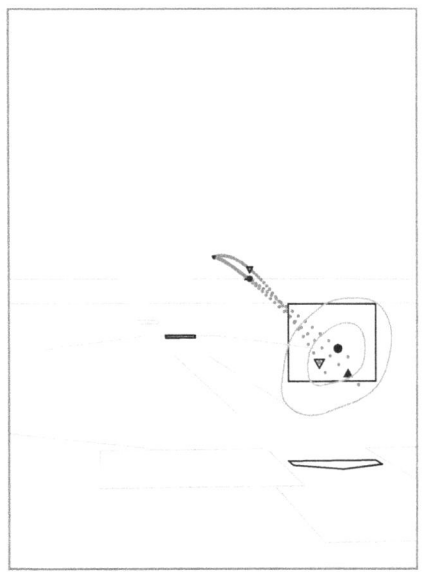

Type	Frequency	Velocity	H Movement	V Movement
● Fastball	39.8%	93.7 [104]	14.4 [66]	-17.8 [95]
□ Sinker				
+ Cutter				
▲ Changeup	17.4%	87.3 [107]	16.9 [73]	-26.3 [103]
× Splitter				
▽ Slider	42.8%	84.7 [101]	-5.4 [102]	-34 [97]
◇ Curveball				
⊕ Slow Curveball				
✳ Knuckleball				
▼ Screwball				

San Francisco Giants 2020

Kevin Gausman   RHP

Born: 01/06/91   Age: 29   Bats: L   Throws: R
Height: 6'3"   Weight: 190   Origin: Round 1, 2012 Draft (#4 overall)

YEAR	TEAM	LVL	AGE	W	L	SV	G	GS	IP	H	HR	BB/9	K/9	K	GB%	BABIP
2017	BAL	MLB	26	11	12	0	34	34	186²	208	29	3.4	8.6	179	44%	.336
2018	BAL	MLB	27	5	8	0	21	21	124	139	21	2.3	7.5	104	48%	.317
2018	ATL	MLB	27	5	3	0	10	10	59²	50	5	2.7	6.6	44	43%	.260
2019	GWN	AAA	28	0	1	0	1	1	7	6	1	1.3	12.9	10	69%	.333
2019	ATL	MLB	28	3	7	0	16	16	80	92	12	3.0	9.6	85	40%	.345
2019	CIN	MLB	28	0	2	0	15	1	22¹	21	3	2.0	11.7	29	45%	.340
2020	SFN	MLB	29	6	8	0	23	23	113	111	15	3.1	9.4	119	44%	.311

Comparables: Joe Ross, Jake Odorizzi, Alex Cobb

Throughout Gausman's time with the Orioles, he generally performed like an above-average starter (making him an ace by Baltimore's low standards), but often flashed the potential for more. Freed from the Birds at the 2018 deadline, he pitched better during his initial run with the Braves. Yet Gausman found himself on the move again last season after a rough go at it that coincided with a foot injury, landing with the Reds via waiver claim. With Cincinnati, he essentially turned into a two-pitch reliever—an effective one at that. Granted, it was only 22 innings, but they were very good innings wherein he fiddled around with throwing his splitter close to 50 percent of the time. The thought of a full year of health and splitter-spamming enticed the Giants into signing him to an incentive-laden one-year deal.

YEAR	TEAM	LVL	AGE	WHIP	ERA	DRA	WARP	MPH	FB%	WHF	CSP
2017	BAL	MLB	26	1.49	4.68	4.91	1.4	97.7	64.3	12	44.9
2018	BAL	MLB	27	1.38	4.43	4.42	1.3	97.1	58.8	12.1	47.2
2018	ATL	MLB	27	1.14	2.87	3.13	1.5	96.5	56.9	12.1	45.9
2019	GWN	AAA	28	1.00	2.57	2.62	0.3				
2019	ATL	MLB	28	1.49	6.19	5.17	0.4	96.7	56.6	14.8	46.1
2019	CIN	MLB	28	1.16	4.03	2.82	0.7	96.8	56.4	20.8	43.1
2020	SFN	MLB	29	1.32	3.78	4.37	1.8	96.4	59.8	13.1	45.8

Kevin Gausman, continued

Pitch Shape vs LHH

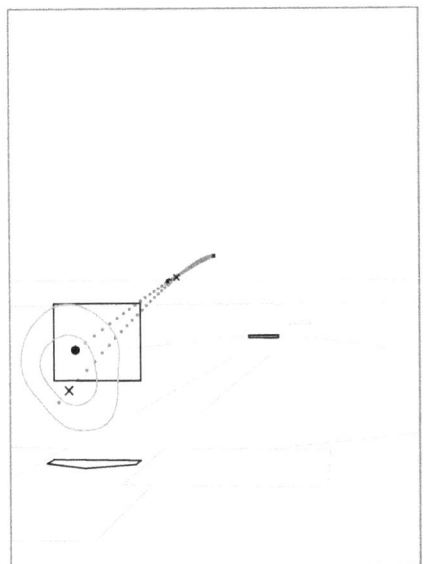

Pitch Shape vs RHH

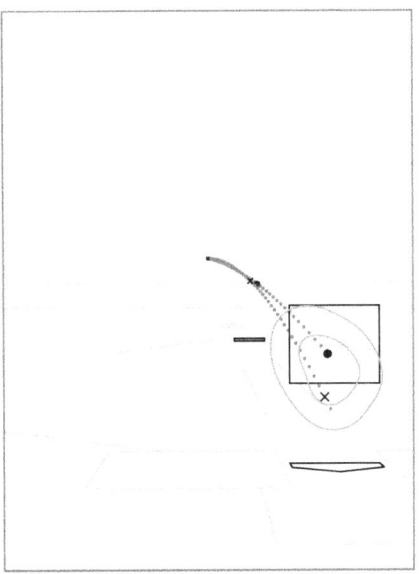

Type	Frequency	Velocity	H Movement	V Movement
● Fastball	56.5%	94.1 [105]	-9.3 [89]	-13.8 [106]
☐ Sinker				
+ Cutter				
▲ Changeup				
✕ Splitter	40.3%	83.6 [94]	-11.7 [86]	-30.9 [94]
▽ Slider				
◇ Curveball				
⊕ Slow Curveball				
✻ Knuckleball				
▼ Screwball				

Trevor Gott RHP

Born: 08/26/92 Age: 27 Bats: R Throws: R
Height: 6'0" Weight: 185 Origin: Round 6, 2013 Draft (#178 overall)

YEAR	TEAM	LVL	AGE	W	L	SV	G	GS	IP	H	HR	BB/9	K/9	K	GB%	BABIP
2017	SYR	AAA	24	2	0	4	30	0	37^1	39	2	3.1	8.4	35	59%	.327
2017	WAS	MLB	24	1	0	0	4	0	3	11	1	9.0	9.0	3	35%	.625
2018	SYR	AAA	25	1	1	3	28	0	29^1	23	1	2.5	11.7	38	56%	.319
2018	WAS	MLB	25	0	2	0	20	0	19	19	4	4.7	7.1	15	58%	.283
2019	SFN	MLB	26	7	0	1	50	0	52^2	41	4	2.9	9.7	57	44%	.276
2020	SFN	MLB	27	3	3	0	56	0	59	58	8	3.2	8.6	57	43%	.301

Comparables: Andrew Bellatti, Sam Tuivailala, Jimmy Herget

One of the hot "new" trends in baseball is the death of the sinker. Pitchers and teams are, en masse, leaving the pitch in the dust in favor of designed pitches that do not allow opposing hitters to elevate low pitches and park them in the bleachers. Gott, a castoff from a Nationals bullpen only charitably described as bad prior to the 2019 season, started his first year with the Giants throwing a four-seam fastball instead of a sinker, and the results were exciting. Now, instead of another year where he appears in this book only due to an eminently pun-able last name, Gott gets a chance to be a late-inning relief option if he can avoid the elbow troubles that sidelined him in August.

YEAR	TEAM	LVL	AGE	WHIP	ERA	DRA	WARP	MPH	FB%	WHF	CSP
2017	SYR	AAA	24	1.39	3.86	4.67	0.3				
2017	WAS	MLB	24	4.67	30.00	10.51	-0.2	96.6	67	9	42.5
2018	SYR	AAA	25	1.06	3.68	3.26	0.6				
2018	WAS	MLB	25	1.53	5.68	6.11	-0.3	96.9	74.8	6.6	52.6
2019	SFN	MLB	26	1.10	4.44	3.86	0.9	96.3	77.2	11.6	49.1
2020	SFN	MLB	27	1.34	3.90	4.48	0.6	96.0	77.1	10.6	49.2

Trevor Gott, continued

Pitch Shape vs LHH

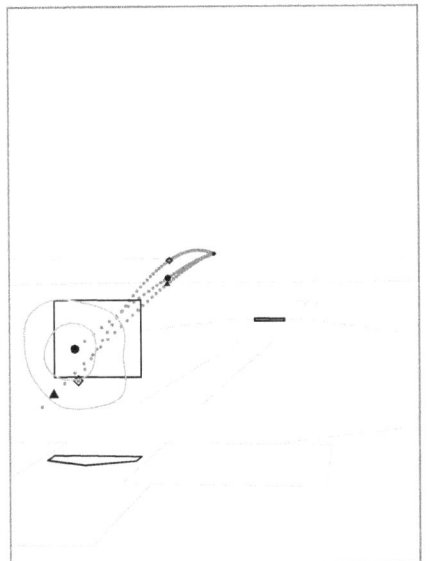

Pitch Shape vs RHH

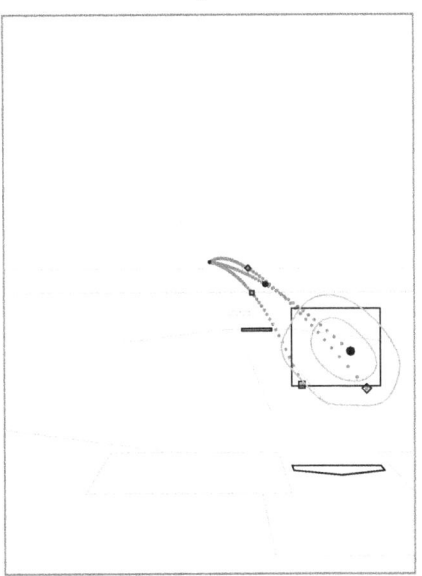

Type	Frequency	Velocity	H Movement	V Movement
● Fastball	66.9%	95 [107]	-6.7 [101]	-14.9 [103]
□ Sinker	10.3%	94.7 [111]	-13.2 [96]	-19.6 [103]
+ Cutter				
▲ Changeup	3.6%	89.3 [115]	-13 [91]	-27.1 [101]
× Splitter				
▽ Slider				
◇ Curveball	17.6%	81.4 [109]	10 [110]	-46 [103]
⊕ Slow Curveball				
✳ Knuckleball				
▼ Screwball				

Jandel Gustave RHP

Born: 10/12/92 Age: 27 Bats: R Throws: R
Height: 6'2" Weight: 210 Origin: International Free Agent, 2010

YEAR	TEAM	LVL	AGE	W	L	SV	G	GS	IP	H	HR	BB/9	K/9	K	GB%	BABIP
2017	HOU	MLB	24	0	0	0	6	0	5	5	0	12.6	3.6	2	50%	.312
2019	SAC	AAA	26	2	2	7	29	1	26¹	28	5	4.1	8.5	25	46%	.307
2019	SFN	MLB	26	0	0	1	23	0	24¹	18	1	3.3	5.2	14	45%	.227
2020	*SFN*	*MLB*	*27*	*2*	*2*	*0*	*45*	*0*	*47*	*50*	*7*	*3.7*	*7.6*	*40*	*45%*	*.308*

Comparables: Sam Tuivailala, Jake Barrett, Daniel Webb

For relief pitchers these days, premium velocity is no longer a differentiator—it's the jump off. So while Gustave can touch triple digits and used that heat to find a place to settle after his 2018 Tommy John surgery rehab, he still needs to find another gear in order to nail down a definite bullpen role. His 2019 performance might've helped, but it also might have been a trick of the light; he hasn't yet converted his velo into whiffs, and his low ERA belies the three "unearned" runs he allowed in September. No, what he needs to stand out is consistency with his slider. If that offering goes back to being a plus pitch, he could find solid ground in the seventh or eighth inning; until then he's best suited to trying to force his heater past hitters in the fifth or the sixth frame.

YEAR	TEAM	LVL	AGE	WHIP	ERA	DRA	WARP	MPH	FB%	WHF	CSP
2017	HOU	MLB	24	2.40	5.40	6.53	-0.1	98.5	57	7.5	48.2
2019	SAC	AAA	26	1.52	6.15	4.59	0.4				
2019	SFN	MLB	26	1.11	2.96	5.76	-0.1	97.9	71.6	9.7	55.4
2020	*SFN*	*MLB*	*27*	*1.47*	*4.82*	*5.25*	*0.1*	*97.5*	*70.2*	*9.5*	*53.3*

Jandel Gustave, continued

Pitch Shape vs LHH **Pitch Shape vs RHH**

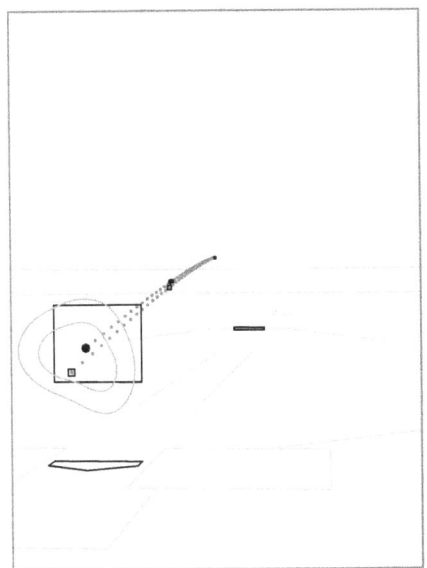 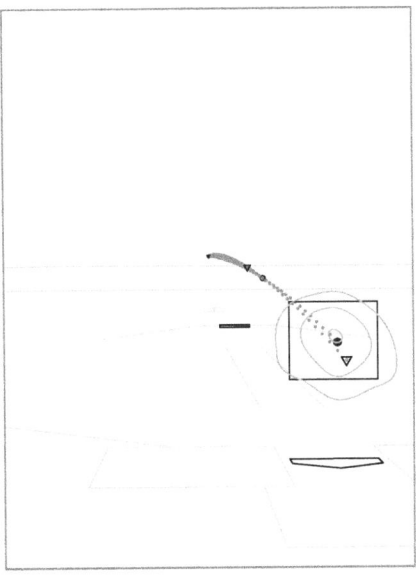

Type	Frequency	Velocity	H Movement	V Movement
● Fastball	53.3%	96.2 [111]	-8 [95]	-15.6 [101]
☐ Sinker	18.3%	96 [118]	-13.4 [95]	-20.8 [99]
+ Cutter				
▲ Changeup				
✕ Splitter				
▽ Slider	28.4%	85.4 [104]	6.8 [107]	-33.5 [99]
◇ Curveball				
✦ Slow Curveball				
✱ Knuckleball				
▼ Screwball				

Reyes Moronta   RHP
Born: 01/06/93   Age: 27   Bats: R   Throws: R
Height: 5'11"   Weight: 241   Origin: International Free Agent, 2011

YEAR	TEAM	LVL	AGE	W	L	SV	G	GS	IP	H	HR	BB/9	K/9	K	GB%	BABIP
2017	RIC	AA	24	0	1	5	19	0	18	15	1	6.0	13.0	26	42%	.333
2017	SAC	AAA	24	3	0	0	13	0	17	13	1	4.2	9.0	17	33%	.273
2017	SFN	MLB	24	0	0	0	7	0	6²	6	1	4.1	14.9	11	47%	.357
2018	SFN	MLB	25	5	2	1	69	0	65	34	4	5.1	10.9	79	43%	.211
2019	SFN	MLB	26	3	7	0	56	0	56²	41	4	5.2	11.1	70	39%	.272
2020	SFN	MLB	27	1	1	0	17	0	18	14	2	4.8	11.7	23	40%	.291

Comparables: Chris Withrow, Carl Edwards Jr., Domingo Germán

Plenty of things made Moronta an outlier in the Giants' bullpen; for one, he'd been fairly consistent through most of the past two seasons, an oddity in one of baseball's most volatile bullpen mixes. Of course there's his stature, with Moronta cutting a shorter and stouter profile than most relievers while still delivering the high-end velocity and a dynamic slider expected of late-inning arms. But more than most, what set Moronta apart was how exciting he was to watch. There was a bit of the cardiac-closer in him, but more Fernando Rodney than Armando Benítez; he tended to walk too many, but a strikeout and the end of an inning was always just a couple heaters away. Unfortunately labrum repair surgery has Moronta unlikely to return to the team until the very end of the 2020 season, so the Giants faithful will have to find another way to enjoy the late innings in the meantime.

YEAR	TEAM	LVL	AGE	WHIP	ERA	DRA	WARP	MPH	FB%	WHF	CSP
2017	RIC	AA	24	1.50	4.00	3.72	0.2				
2017	SAC	AAA	24	1.24	2.12	3.16	0.4				
2017	SFN	MLB	24	1.35	2.70	2.60	0.2	97.8	52.7	16.4	50.2
2018	SFN	MLB	25	1.09	2.49	3.09	1.4	99.0	51	14.8	47.2
2019	SFN	MLB	26	1.31	2.86	4.10	0.8	98.9	58.3	12.5	45.4
2020	SFN	MLB	27	1.33	3.45	4.01	0.3	98.4	55.5	13.8	47.8

Reyes Moronta, continued

Pitch Shape vs LHH

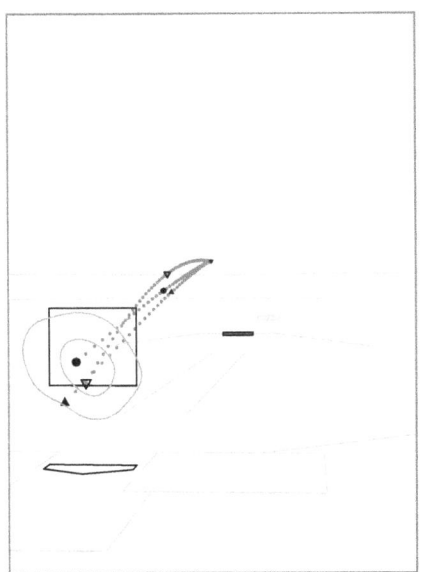

Pitch Shape vs RHH

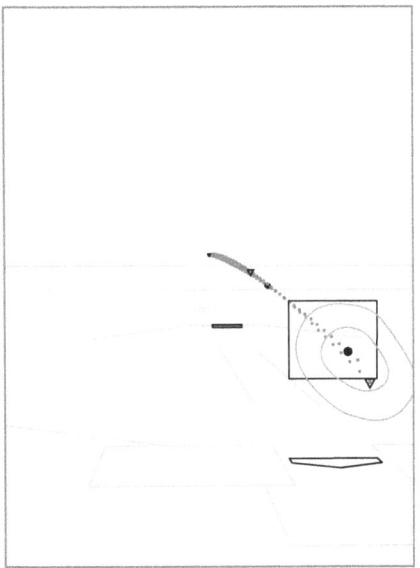

Type	Frequency	Velocity	H Movement	V Movement
● Fastball	58.3%	97.6 [115]	-4.5 [110]	-11.6 [111]
□ Sinker				
+ Cutter				
▲ Changeup	7.0%	90.2 [118]	-15.3 [80]	-24.4 [109]
× Splitter				
▽ Slider	34.7%	83.7 [97]	11.3 [126]	-33.5 [99]
◇ Curveball				
⊕ Slow Curveball				
✳ Knuckleball				
▼ Screwball				

Dereck Rodríguez RHP

Born: 06/05/92 Age: 28 Bats: R Throws: R
Height: 6'1" Weight: 215 Origin: Round 6, 2011 Draft (#208 overall)

YEAR	TEAM	LVL	AGE	W	L	SV	G	GS	IP	H	HR	BB/9	K/9	K	GB%	BABIP
2017	FTM	A+	25	5	2	0	11	11	68	59	7	1.5	7.8	59	43%	.278
2017	CHT	AA	25	5	4	0	15	13	75^1	74	9	3.2	7.4	62	41%	.294
2018	SAC	AAA	26	4	1	0	9	9	50^1	49	11	2.0	9.5	53	39%	.284
2018	SFN	MLB	26	6	4	0	21	19	118^1	98	9	2.7	6.8	89	41%	.257
2019	SAC	AAA	27	3	0	0	6	6	29^2	26	4	3.0	8.5	28	47%	.278
2019	SFN	MLB	27	6	11	0	28	16	99	108	21	3.3	6.5	71	46%	.282
2020	SFN	MLB	28	5	8	0	39	16	105	110	17	3.2	6.7	78	43%	.292

Comparables: Mark Leiter Jr., Brock Stewart, Luis Santos

Eyed as an obvious regression candidate from his solid 2018 rookie season, Rodríguez couldn't hang onto his starting rotation slot consistently last year, and was pushed to the bullpen and to Triple-A as the Giants looked to find ways to give others the shot Rodríguez made so much of once. In the end, it might be as simple as this: He just doesn't have the velocity or movement on his pitches to get outs consistently. Despite command and four pitches, he gets hammered when allowed to face hitters a second or third time, perhaps in part to all the pitches he has to throw his first time through. As one of the most ineffective semi-regular starting pitchers in baseball last year, he'll have to continue to work on refining his offerings and getting more movement, or else find himself resigned to a swingman role or toiling in the PCL.

YEAR	TEAM	LVL	AGE	WHIP	ERA	DRA	WARP	MPH	FB%	WHF	CSP
2017	FTM	A+	25	1.03	2.51	3.32	1.6				
2017	CHT	AA	25	1.34	3.94	5.39	-0.2				
2018	SAC	AAA	26	1.19	3.40	3.53	1.1				
2018	SFN	MLB	26	1.13	2.81	5.18	0.1	94.6	53.3	9.9	48
2019	SAC	AAA	27	1.21	3.64	2.85	1.1				
2019	SFN	MLB	27	1.45	5.64	6.69	-1.1	93.2	48.6	9.5	46.7
2020	SFN	MLB	28	1.40	4.58	5.17	0.7	93.3	51.1	9.8	47.6

Dereck Rodríguez, continued

Pitch Shape vs LHH

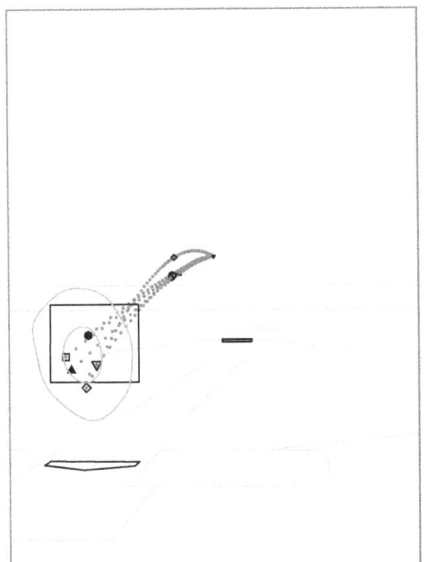

Pitch Shape vs RHH

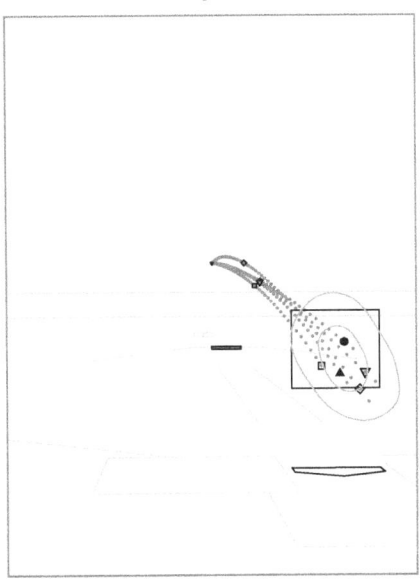

Type	Frequency	Velocity	H Movement	V Movement
● Fastball	39.4%	91.2 [97]	-2.7 [119]	-15.1 [102]
□ Sinker	9.3%	90 [86]	-10.2 [116]	-17.9 [109]
+ Cutter				
▲ Changeup	20.7%	84.8 [99]	-11.9 [97]	-24.8 [108]
× Splitter				
▽ Slider	13.8%	86.9 [111]	3.2 [92]	-25.5 [122]
◇ Curveball	16.9%	76 [91]	10.9 [114]	-54.2 [86]
✦ Slow Curveball				
✳ Knuckleball				
▼ Screwball				

Giants Player Analysis - 77

Tyler Rogers RHP

Born: 12/17/90 Age: 29 Bats: R Throws: R
Height: 6'5" Weight: 187 Origin: Round 10, 2013 Draft (#312 overall)

YEAR	TEAM	LVL	AGE	W	L	SV	G	GS	IP	H	HR	BB/9	K/9	K	GB%	BABIP
2017	SAC	AAA	26	4	4	10	55	0	76	65	2	3.3	5.1	43	63%	.268
2018	SAC	AAA	27	3	2	3	51	0	67^2	50	4	3.1	8.0	60	62%	.254
2019	SAC	AAA	28	4	2	5	49	1	62	59	6	4.1	8.0	55	63%	.306
2019	SFN	MLB	28	2	0	0	17	0	17^2	12	0	1.5	8.2	16	70%	.240
2020	SFN	MLB	29	2	3	3	45	0	47	55	12	2.8	6.2	33	60%	.288

Comparables: Colton Murray, Jose A. Valdez, Jorge Rondon

There's a dominant submariner in San Francisco, and no, Prince Namor hasn't conquered McCovey Cove. After two PCL All-Star game appearances, Rogers was a revelation when he joined the Giants late in 2019, shockingly effective against lefties and righties alike. Of course his unconventional delivery makes for a fan-favorite, but what's even more appealing was the fact that *he was actually pretty good*. Amidst the slapdash relief options the Giants have coming into 2020, Rogers is one of the most likely to worm(burn) his way into the late innings as well as fans' hearts. While there still isn't a huge sample size of major-league performance and his fastball would never get pulled over by CHiPs if it were cruising down I-80, the onus is now on management to let him sink or swim in the bigs.

YEAR	TEAM	LVL	AGE	WHIP	ERA	DRA	WARP	MPH	FB%	WHF	CSP
2017	SAC	AAA	26	1.22	2.37	3.43	1.6				
2018	SAC	AAA	27	1.08	2.13	2.72	1.9				
2019	SAC	AAA	28	1.40	4.21	3.99	1.4				
2019	SFN	MLB	28	0.85	1.02	3.96	0.3	83.7	67.1	8.2	55.2
2020	SFN	MLB	29	1.47	5.63	6.13	-0.4	83.1	67.1	8.2	55.2

Tyler Rogers, continued

Pitch Shape vs LHH

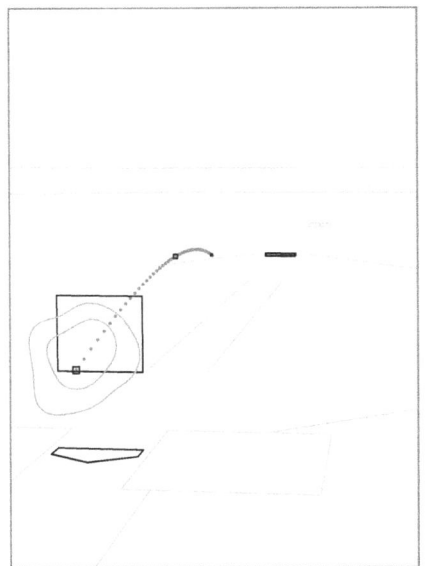

Pitch Shape vs RHH

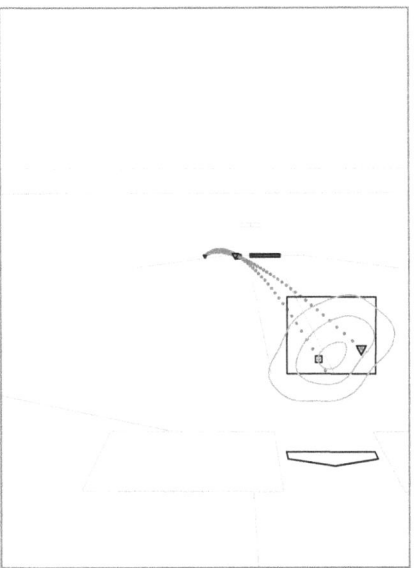

Type	Frequency	Velocity	H Movement	V Movement
● Fastball				
☐ Sinker	67.1%	82.4 [47]	-1.7 [171]	-47.9 [3]
+ Cutter				
▲ Changeup				
✕ Splitter				
▽ Slider	32.9%	72.8 [51]	10.9 [125]	-37.6 [87]
◇ Curveball				
⊕ Slow Curveball				
✻ Knuckleball				
▼ Screwball				

Giants Player Analysis

San Francisco Giants 2020

Tyson Ross RHP

Born: 04/22/87 Age: 33 Bats: R Throws: R
Height: 6'6" Weight: 245 Origin: Round 2, 2008 Draft (#58 overall)

YEAR	TEAM	LVL	AGE	W	L	SV	G	GS	IP	H	HR	BB/9	K/9	K	GB%	BABIP
2017	FRI	AA	30	1	1	0	2	2	11²	11	0	3.1	7.7	10	62%	.324
2017	ROU	AAA	30	2	1	0	4	4	18²	23	3	5.3	5.3	11	46%	.345
2017	TEX	MLB	30	3	3	0	12	10	49	53	7	6.8	6.6	36	48%	.305
2018	SDN	MLB	31	6	9	0	22	22	123¹	112	16	3.8	7.8	107	45%	.276
2018	SLN	MLB	31	2	0	0	9	1	26¹	20	1	3.4	5.1	15	58%	.244
2019	DET	MLB	32	1	5	0	7	7	35¹	41	7	4.6	6.4	25	51%	.306
2020	SFN	MLB	33	2	2	0	33	0	35	36	6	3.9	7.7	30	47%	.294

Comparables: Andrew Cashner, Lance Lynn, Jake Arrieta

A recent CareerBuilder survey said that 75 percent of hiring managers have found a lie on a résumé. The only one that slipped through the human resources fact-checkers was Ross claiming he was the All-Star representative for the Padres in 2014. Unfortunately, there is no way to verify that. An All-Star appearance, especially for a starting pitcher, gives you about five extra fliers for your career. Ross has a couple left after a tectonically turbulent Tigers season, missing his spots when he wasn't missing in action.

YEAR	TEAM	LVL	AGE	WHIP	ERA	DRA	WARP	MPH	FB%	WHF	CSP
2017	FRI	AA	30	1.29	2.31	4.50	0.1				
2017	ROU	AAA	30	1.82	7.71	7.55	-0.4				
2017	TEX	MLB	30	1.84	7.71	8.24	-1.5	94.1	57.1	7.7	41.1
2018	SDN	MLB	31	1.33	4.45	4.94	0.5	93.5	41.7	9.3	43.9
2018	SLN	MLB	31	1.14	2.73	5.50	-0.1	94.2	41.7	8.3	46.1
2019	DET	MLB	32	1.67	6.11	7.59	-0.7	92.1	46.3	7.2	46.1
2020	SFN	MLB	33	1.45	5.04	5.03	0.1	92.4	44.8	8.4	43.7

Tyson Ross, continued

Pitch Shape vs LHH

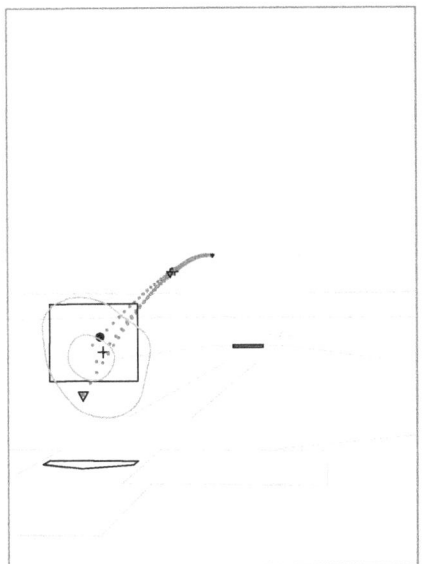

Pitch Shape vs RHH

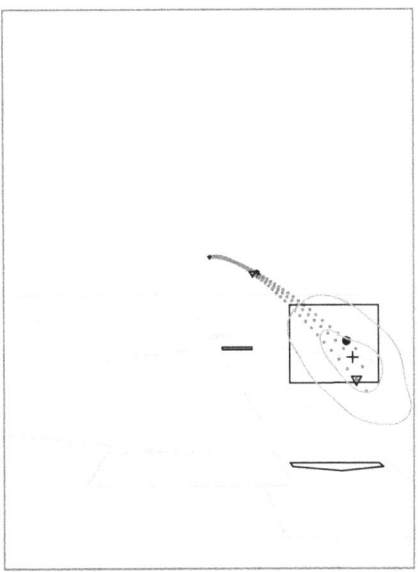

Type	Frequency	Velocity	H Movement	V Movement
● Fastball	45.8%	90.4 [94]	1.1 [135]	-21.5 [86]
☐ Sinker				
+ Cutter	25.1%	88.8 [101]	1.7 [99]	-25.8 [94]
▲ Changeup				
✕ Splitter				
▽ Slider	28.3%	84.2 [99]	5.6 [103]	-36.3 [91]
◇ Curveball				
✦ Slow Curveball				
✱ Knuckleball				
▼ Screwball				

Giants Player Analysis - 81

Jeff Samardzija RHP

Born: 01/23/85 Age: 35 Bats: R Throws: R
Height: 6'5" Weight: 240 Origin: Round 5, 2006 Draft (#149 overall)

YEAR	TEAM	LVL	AGE	W	L	SV	G	GS	IP	H	HR	BB/9	K/9	K	GB%	BABIP
2017	SFN	MLB	32	9	15	0	32	32	207^2	204	30	1.4	8.9	205	43%	.303
2018	SAC	AAA	33	0	2	0	4	4	17	17	5	1.6	10.6	20	40%	.286
2018	SFN	MLB	33	1	5	0	10	10	44^2	47	6	5.2	6.0	30	32%	.287
2019	SFN	MLB	34	11	12	0	32	32	181^1	152	28	2.4	6.9	140	37%	.240
2020	SFN	MLB	35	8	10	0	26	26	148	144	25	2.4	7.2	118	37%	.276

Comparables: Jake Arrieta, Ian Kennedy, Wade Davis

While it's not fair to say that everything went right during Samardzija's bounceback season, the veteran righty did seem a bit charmed last year. For years he's been a serial home-run-allower, but this season only seven of the 28 he allowed plated more than one run. (His career solo homer percentage is 60 percent, so that's a marked improvement.) In addition, he had the second-lowest BABIP among qualified starting pitchers, behind only AL Cy Young Justin Verlander. All this helped keep his ERA tidy despite a strikeout rate that matched his ill-fated season on the South Side of Chicago. The Shark now swims into the final season of his contract as a useful member of the roster: a reliable mid-rotation starter who may be able to fetch a return in trade despite his hefty contract.

YEAR	TEAM	LVL	AGE	WHIP	ERA	DRA	WARP	MPH	FB%	WHF	CSP
2017	SFN	MLB	32	1.14	4.42	3.43	5.0	96.7	56.8	11.1	50.5
2018	SAC	AAA	33	1.18	5.29	4.27	0.2				
2018	SFN	MLB	33	1.63	6.25	7.20	-1.0	96.0	63.2	9.2	46.3
2019	SFN	MLB	34	1.11	3.52	4.40	2.7	94.1	68.9	9.7	47.8
2020	SFN	MLB	35	1.25	3.94	4.69	1.9	94.0	62.9	9.9	47.1

Jeff Samardzija, continued

Pitch Shape vs LHH

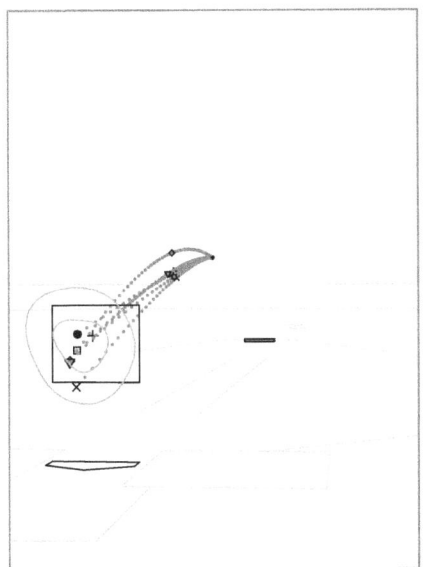

Pitch Shape vs RHH

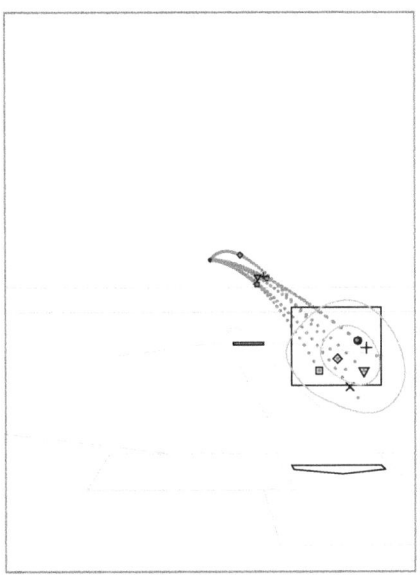

Type	Frequency	Velocity	H Movement	V Movement
● Fastball	26.7%	91.9 [99]	-8.4 [93]	-15.2 [102]
□ Sinker	19.5%	92.5 [99]	-14.2 [90]	-20.4 [100]
+ Cutter	22.7%	89.3 [104]	-1.6 [80]	-20.2 [114]
▲ Changeup				
× Splitter	8.2%	82.6 [89]	-6 [107]	-27.1 [107]
▽ Slider	20.3%	85.5 [105]	-0.3 [78]	-27.1 [117]
◇ Curveball				
◈ Slow Curveball				
✱ Knuckleball				
▼ Screwball				

Sam Selman LHP

Born: 11/14/90 Age: 29 Bats: R Throws: L
Height: 6'3" Weight: 190 Origin: Round 2, 2012 Draft (#66 overall)

YEAR	TEAM	LVL	AGE	W	L	SV	G	GS	IP	H	HR	BB/9	K/9	K	GB%	BABIP
2017	NWA	AA	26	4	3	5	24	0	39^1	21	1	4.3	13.5	59	38%	.260
2017	OMA	AAA	26	0	1	3	18	0	28^1	13	1	6.0	12.1	38	35%	.214
2018	NWA	AA	27	1	2	0	12	0	12^1	12	0	8.0	15.3	21	37%	.444
2018	OMA	AAA	27	0	2	0	23	0	28^1	22	0	6.0	11.8	37	45%	.328
2019	RIC	AA	28	0	0	0	4	0	7	3	0	1.3	16.7	13	58%	.250
2019	SAC	AAA	28	3	2	0	39	1	48	25	4	3.0	15.2	81	41%	.253
2019	SFN	MLB	28	0	0	0	10	0	10^1	6	2	5.2	8.7	10	38%	.167
2020	SFN	MLB	29	2	2	0	34	0	36	32	8	4.0	8.8	35	39%	.262

Comparables: Hunter Cervenka, Austin Adams, Ryan Mattheus

A move from Omaha to Sacramento—with a stop at Driveline Baseball to work on his mechanics—was just what Selman needed after years toiling in the upper minors for the Royals. He was a revelation for his new PCL squad, and appeared to have finally overcome his walk issues while posting the highest strikeout rate in the league among pitchers with more than 25 innings pitched. Called up after the Giants' post-deadline bullpen exodus, Selman might have forgotten to pack his control; he was beat up after being used almost equally against righties and lefties. If he can keep his mechanics consistent and, consequently, his pitches close to the zone, expect to see his vicious slider in high-leverage innings in 2020.

YEAR	TEAM	LVL	AGE	WHIP	ERA	DRA	WARP	MPH	FB%	WHF	CSP
2017	NWA	AA	26	1.02	2.97	2.34	1.2				
2017	OMA	AAA	26	1.13	2.22	2.81	0.8				
2018	NWA	AA	27	1.86	6.57	4.19	0.1				
2018	OMA	AAA	27	1.45	4.13	3.55	0.5				
2019	RIC	AA	28	0.57	0.00	2.23	0.2				
2019	SAC	AAA	28	0.85	2.06	0.69	2.6				
2019	SFN	MLB	28	1.16	4.35	5.45	0.0	92.2	42.5	12.4	43.1
2020	SFN	MLB	29	1.36	4.51	5.18	0.1	91.6	42.5	12.4	43.1

Sam Selman, *continued*

Pitch Shape vs LHH   *Pitch Shape vs RHH*

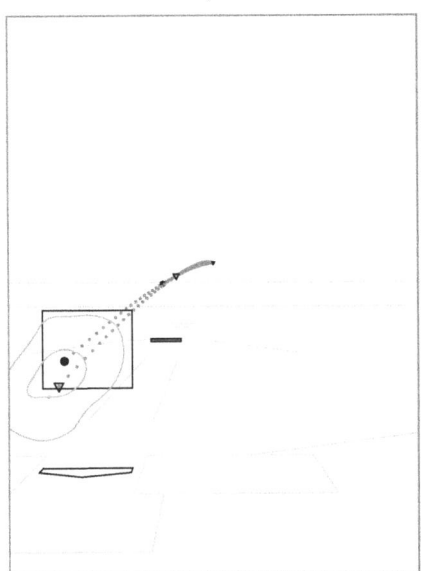 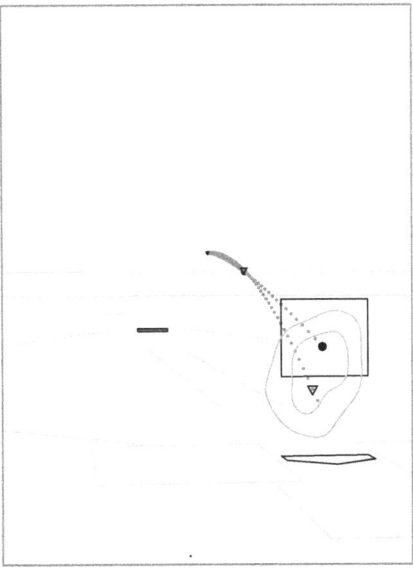

Type	Frequency	Velocity	H Movement	V Movement
● Fastball	42.5%	90 [93]	2 [121]	-18 [95]
☐ Sinker				
+ Cutter				
▲ Changeup				
✕ Splitter				
▽ Slider	57.5%	79.9 [81]	-10.7 [124]	-35.9 [92]
◇ Curveball				
⊕ Slow Curveball				
✳ Knuckleball				
▼ Screwball				

Giants Player Analysis - 85

Drew Smyly LHP

Born: 06/13/89 Age: 31 Bats: L Throws: L
Height: 6'3" Weight: 190 Origin: Round 2, 2010 Draft (#68 overall)

YEAR	TEAM	LVL	AGE	W	L	SV	G	GS	IP	H	HR	BB/9	K/9	K	GB%	BABIP
2019	SAN	AAA	30	1	0	0	3	3	12^2	10	2	2.1	12.8	18	31%	.296
2019	TEX	MLB	30	1	5	1	13	9	51^1	64	19	6.0	9.1	52	29%	.310
2019	PHI	MLB	30	3	2	0	12	12	62^2	62	13	3.0	9.8	68	40%	.306
2020	PHI	MLB	31	2	2	0	33	0	35	35	8	3.6	8.9	35	34%	.291

Comparables: Steven Matz, David Price, Matt Moore

Recency bias is usually presented within a positive framework, part of a euphoric panacea that makes us collectively forget the bad times for a player or team that previously occurred. In Smyly's case, the past three years have been such a nightmarish rollercoaster that it's easy to forget he had a 3.24 ERA in his first 395 professional innings. Smyly finally stepped on a major-league mound after nearly two full years of recovery and rehab from Tommy John surgery, but was a punching bag in Texas before becoming a barely serviceable back-end starter in Philadelphia. Velocity was never Smyly's game, so slight uptick in his fastball did little if anything for his cause. Unfortunately, fly balls have always been a part of his game as well—which has been more of a bug than a feature in the rabbit ball era.

YEAR	TEAM	LVL	AGE	WHIP	ERA	DRA	WARP	MPH	FB%	WHF	CSP
2019	SAN	AAA	30	1.03	4.97	2.50	0.5				
2019	TEX	MLB	30	1.91	8.42	9.68	-2.2	92.8	43.1	10	48.9
2019	PHI	MLB	30	1.32	4.45	5.10	0.4	93.3	43.1	12.8	44.1
2020	PHI	MLB	31	1.41	5.13	5.17	0.1	92.2	42.9	11.3	46.2

Drew Smyly, continued

Pitch Shape vs LHH

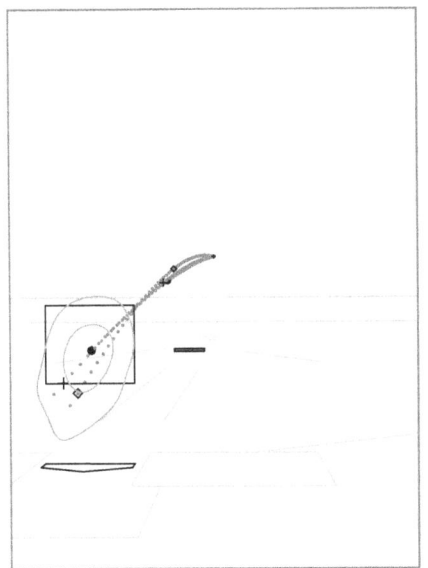

Pitch Shape vs RHH

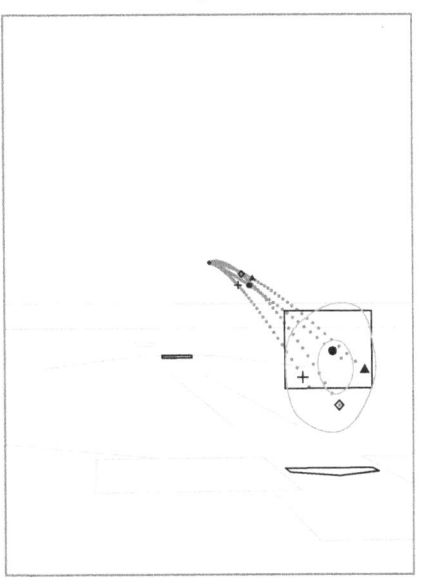

Type	Frequency	Velocity	H Movement	V Movement
● Fastball	47.9%	91.4 [97]	4.9 [109]	-12.8 [108]
□ Sinker				
+ Cutter	18.1%	86.9 [89]	1.8 [79]	-23.1 [104]
▲ Changeup	4.8%	82.7 [91]	2.9 [139]	-23.4 [112]
✕ Splitter				
▽ Slider				
◇ Curveball	29.2%	77.6 [97]	3.9 [54]	-42.3 [111]
⊕ Slow Curveball				
✳ Knuckleball				
▼ Screwball				

San Francisco Giants 2020

Nick Vincent RHP

Born: 07/12/86   Age: 33   Bats: R   Throws: R
Height: 6'0"   Weight: 185   Origin: Round 18, 2008 Draft (#555 overall)

YEAR	TEAM	LVL	AGE	W	L	SV	G	GS	IP	H	HR	BB/9	K/9	K	GB%	BABIP
2017	SEA	MLB	30	3	3	0	69	0	64²	62	3	1.8	7.0	50	35%	.301
2018	SEA	MLB	31	4	4	0	62	1	56¹	50	7	2.4	8.9	56	31%	.272
2019	LEH	AAA	32	0	0	0	10	0	12¹	9	1	0.7	9.5	13	35%	.242
2019	SFN	MLB	32	0	2	0	18	1	30²	36	7	2.3	8.8	30	39%	.322
2019	PHI	MLB	32	1	2	0	14	0	14	11	1	2.6	10.9	17	35%	.303
2020	PHI	MLB	33	2	2	0	33	0	35	33	6	2.1	8.5	33	34%	.281

Comparables: Huston Street, Fernando Salas, Bruce Sutter

If necessity is the mother of invention, Philadelphia's front office was an old timey frontier doctor delivering little miracles in the back of the bullpen. The Phillies used 27 relievers in 2019, which doesn't even include the three position players the team trudged to the hill when games were well out of hand. Limited to 18 outings with the Giants due to a pectoral injury in May, the Phils signed Vincent as a free agent in August after the Giants cut him. Vincent was his usual effective albeit boring self, throwing a low-90s fastball and upper-80s cutter at the top of the zone and somehow getting results. In a season where the Phillies bullpen was more crowded than the Duggar household, Vincent was one of the forgotten middle children who seldom gets mentioned after Season 3.

YEAR	TEAM	LVL	AGE	WHIP	ERA	DRA	WARP	MPH	FB%	WHF	CSP
2017	SEA	MLB	30	1.16	3.20	4.11	0.8	91.5	94.4	11.2	49.3
2018	SEA	MLB	31	1.15	3.99	3.55	0.9	91.3	96	13.2	50.9
2019	LEH	AAA	32	0.81	1.46	2.33	0.5				
2019	SFN	MLB	32	1.43	5.58	5.66	-0.1	90.6	94.8	12.7	48.5
2019	PHI	MLB	32	1.07	1.93	4.00	0.2	90.2	94.8	11.1	51.9
2020	PHI	MLB	33	1.18	4.00	4.23	0.5	90.1	93.9	12.1	49.3

Nick Vincent, continued

Pitch Shape vs LHH

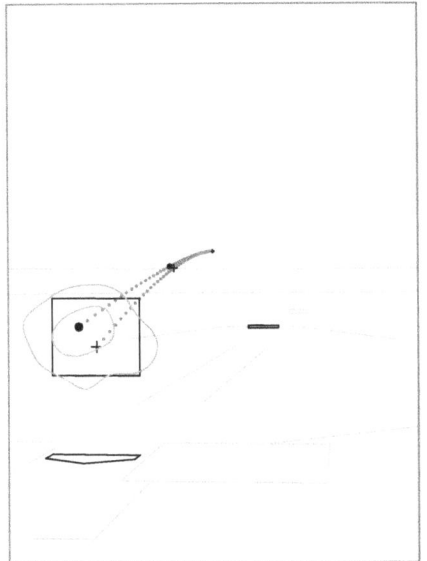

Pitch Shape vs RHH

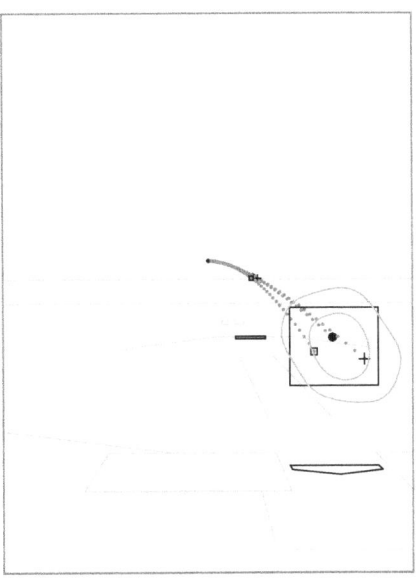

Type	Frequency	Velocity	H Movement	V Movement
● Fastball	51.1%	89.4 [91]	-3.5 [115]	-15.9 [100]
□ Sinker	4.7%	89.6 [84]	-11.6 [107]	-20.4 [100]
+ Cutter	39.4%	87.4 [92]	2.3 [103]	-21.8 [108]
▲ Changeup	3.8%	84 [95]	-13.6 [88]	-28.1 [98]
✕ Splitter				
▽ Slider				
◇ Curveball				
✦ Slow Curveball				
✳ Knuckleball				
▼ Screwball				

Giants Player Analysis

Tony Watson LHP

Born: 05/30/85   Age: 35   Bats: L   Throws: L
Height: 6'3"   Weight: 218   Origin: Round 9, 2007 Draft (#278 overall)

YEAR	TEAM	LVL	AGE	W	L	SV	G	GS	IP	H	HR	BB/9	K/9	K	GB%	BABIP
2017	PIT	MLB	32	5	3	10	47	0	46²	57	7	2.7	6.8	35	46%	.333
2017	LAN	MLB	32	2	1	0	24	0	20	15	2	2.7	8.1	18	62%	.241
2018	SFN	MLB	33	4	6	0	72	0	66	54	4	1.9	9.8	72	47%	.294
2019	SFN	MLB	34	2	2	0	60	0	54	56	9	2.0	6.8	41	46%	.287
2020	SFN	MLB	35	3	3	13	56	0	59	57	9	2.4	8.3	55	47%	.289

Comparables: Fernando Abad, Mike Stanton, Jerry Blevins

Ironically dubbed an "especially nimble" reliever in last year's Annual due to his ability to thrive in almost any relief situation, Watson didn't look too agile breaking his wrist while diving to make a tag on Kolten Wong and preserve a win last September. (He'd later describe his move as "lay out like a 34-year-old dad," which was harsh but fair.) Paired with a disappointing '19 campaign, it's no big surprise that he exercised his player option to remain with the Giants instead of making another questionable leap, this time into free agency. Beyond his collection of talents which include adaptability, resilience, late-inning experience and a (mostly) functional left arm, the Giants should be especially glad to have a player who had the will to dive and sacrifice his arm to save (but not save) a meaningless September game. Players like Watson, more often than not, tend to land on their feet.

YEAR	TEAM	LVL	AGE	WHIP	ERA	DRA	WARP	MPH	FB%	WHF	CSP
2017	PIT	MLB	32	1.52	3.66	5.55	-0.2	95.2	65.1	14	50.8
2017	LAN	MLB	32	1.05	2.70	5.14	0.0	95.4	64.9	13.3	46.7
2018	SFN	MLB	33	1.03	2.59	3.31	1.2	94.6	51.2	13.9	54.4
2019	SFN	MLB	34	1.26	4.17	5.57	-0.1	94.6	51.5	13.6	49
2020	SFN	MLB	35	1.23	3.63	4.32	0.7	93.5	54.1	13.5	50

Tony Watson, continued

Pitch Shape vs LHH

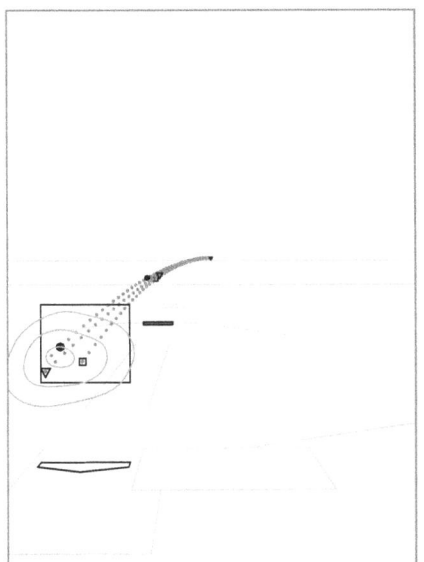

Pitch Shape vs RHH

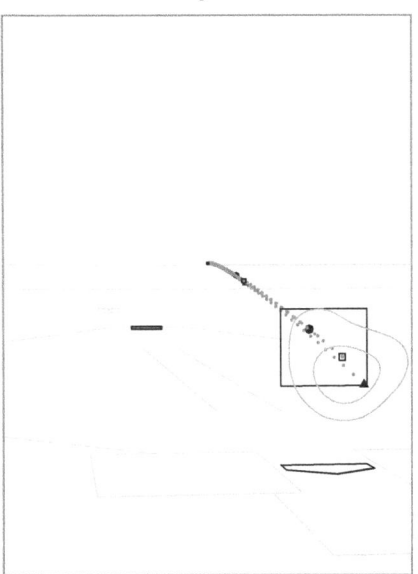

Type	Frequency	Velocity	H Movement	V Movement
● Fastball	17.2%	93.5 [103]	13.1 [72]	-19.4 [91]
☐ Sinker	34.3%	93.1 [102]	15.7 [80]	-21.8 [95]
+ Cutter				
▲ Changeup	37.7%	86.4 [104]	18.2 [67]	-27.5 [100]
✕ Splitter				
▽ Slider	10.8%	85.9 [106]	-1.3 [85]	-28.8 [112]
◇ Curveball				
⊕ Slow Curveball				
✳ Knuckleball				
▼ Screwball				

San Francisco Giants 2020

Logan Webb   RHP

Born: 11/18/96   Age: 23   Bats: R   Throws: R
Height: 6'2"   Weight: 220   Origin: Round 4, 2014 Draft (#118 overall)

YEAR	TEAM	LVL	AGE	W	L	SV	G	GS	IP	H	HR	BB/9	K/9	K	GB%	BABIP
2017	SLO	A-	20	2	0	0	15	0	28	26	1	2.2	10.0	31	68%	.325
2018	SJO	A+	21	1	3	0	21	20	74	54	2	4.4	9.0	74	48%	.274
2018	RIC	AA	21	1	2	0	6	6	30^2	30	4	3.2	7.6	26	52%	.289
2019	AUG	A	22	1	0	0	2	1	10	4	0	2.7	8.1	9	62%	.167
2019	RIC	AA	22	1	4	0	8	7	41^1	41	2	2.6	10.2	47	66%	.333
2019	SAC	AAA	22	0	0	0	1	1	7	7	0	0.0	9.0	7	63%	.368
2019	SFN	MLB	22	2	3	0	8	8	39^2	44	5	3.2	8.4	37	48%	.333
2020	SFN	MLB	23	5	7	0	18	18	89	94	12	3.6	7.7	76	52%	.309

Comparables: Tyler Mahle, Joe Ross, Zack Littell

To say that Webb's year was up-and-down might be underselling the dips and dives of his rookie season. After starting off hot in Double-A and building off his revitalized fastball velocity, Webb earned an 80-game PED suspension that seemed to tie a nice little bow on how his velo jumped up after his return from Tommy John surgery in 2017. After returning he picked up where he left off, posting great performances at *four* levels before finding his way to San Francisco to hold down a starting slot until the season's end. At 22 years old, Webb doesn't have the command or the secondaries (yet) to dominate as a starter, and that showed in his uneven performance at the big-league level. The Giants would probably prefer him to develop in the minors further before plunging him into the big-league fire, but he's already proven he can maintain starting pitcher status.

YEAR	TEAM	LVL	AGE	WHIP	ERA	DRA	WARP	MPH	FB%	WHF	CSP
2017	SLO	A-	20	1.18	2.89	3.49	0.5				
2018	SJO	A+	21	1.22	1.82	3.10	1.9				
2018	RIC	AA	21	1.34	3.82	5.29	0.0				
2019	AUG	A	22	0.70	0.90	3.02	0.2				
2019	RIC	AA	22	1.28	2.18	4.35	0.3				
2019	SAC	AAA	22	1.00	1.29	3.15	0.2				
2019	SFN	MLB	22	1.46	5.22	4.17	0.7	94.6	56.4	9.8	45.5
2020	SFN	MLB	23	1.45	4.40	4.93	0.9	94.5	58.4	10.1	47.1

Logan Webb, continued

Pitch Shape vs LHH

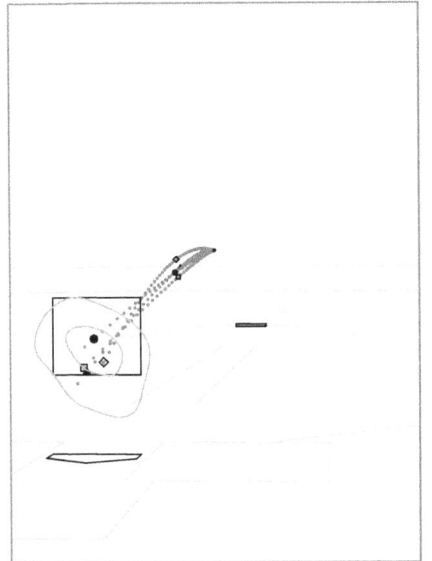

Pitch Shape vs RHH

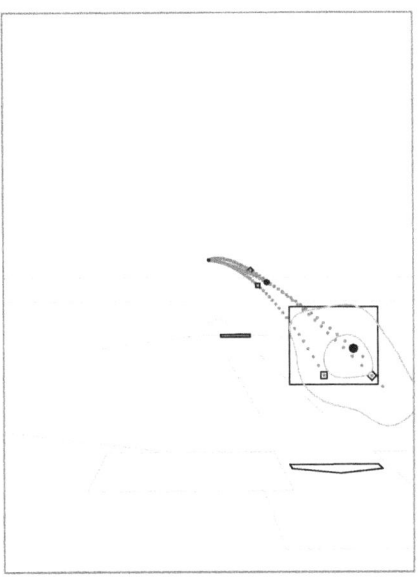

Type	Frequency	Velocity	H Movement	V Movement
● Fastball	42.6%	93.3 [102]	-7.5 [97]	-16 [100]
☐ Sinker	13.8%	92 [97]	-14.3 [89]	-22 [94]
+ Cutter				
▲ Changeup	20.1%	85 [99]	-10.2 [104]	-34.6 [79]
✕ Splitter				
▽ Slider				
◇ Curveball	23.5%	81.9 [111]	10 [110]	-37.8 [121]
✦ Slow Curveball				
✳ Knuckleball				
▼ Screwball				

PLAYER COMMENTS WITHOUT GRAPHS

Abiatal Avelino SS
Born: 02/14/95   Age: 25   Bats: R   Throws: R
Height: 5'11"   Weight: 195   Origin: International Free Agent, 2011

YEAR	TEAM	LVL	AGE	PA	R	2B	3B	HR	RBI	BB	K	SB	CS	AVG/OBP/SLG
2017	TAM	A+	22	34	1	1	0	0	2	2	5	4	0	.219/.265/.250
2017	TRN	AA	22	249	35	12	4	3	28	14	33	4	0	.270/.315/.396
2017	SWB	AAA	22	68	5	1	1	0	6	5	10	3	1	.213/.284/.262
2018	TRN	AA	23	211	32	7	2	10	28	18	37	15	4	.337/.392/.553
2018	SWB	AAA	23	290	33	6	6	5	38	14	61	10	2	.252/.291/.372
2018	SFN	MLB	23	11	1	0	0	0	0	0	3	0	0	.273/.273/.273
2019	SAC	AAA	24	502	70	24	8	12	62	23	84	17	5	.283/.315/.444
2019	SFN	MLB	24	8	0	0	0	0	1	1	3	0	0	.286/.375/.286
2020	SFN	MLB	25	70	6	3	0	1	6	3	15	2	1	.228/.268/.336

Comparables: Yairo Muñoz, Eduardo Escobar, Tim Lopes

The most important thing about Avelino's 2019 season might be that he was able to hold onto some of his 2018 power surge, hitting a dozen homers at Triple-A and supplementing it with "tricky-speedster slugging": eight triples that belied his combination of gap power and foot speed. Here's a speedy, solid defensive infielder with versatility and a little pop on a team that struggled in the infield in 2019 so … naturally Bruce Bochy gave plate appearances to veterans like Donovan Solano, Pablo Sandoval and Cristhian Adames instead. With the Giants perhaps drifting even further into rebuilding mode in 2020, perhaps Avelino will get more chances during this coming year, but he'll likely need to improve his on-base skills to endear himself to Gabe Kapler and establish himself as a regular.

YEAR	TEAM	LVL	AGE	PA	DRC+	VORP	BABIP	BRR	FRAA	WARP
2017	TAM	A+	22	34	64	-0.8	.259	0.6	3B(8): 0.5, 2B(2): 0.0	0.1
2017	TRN	AA	22	249	92	12.6	.301	4.4	2B(39): 1.7, SS(16): 0.5	1.3
2017	SWB	AAA	22	68	58	-1.6	.255	0.1	SS(11): 0.0, 3B(6): -0.4	-0.1
2018	TRN	AA	23	211	161	26.5	.375	-0.2	SS(44): 3.4, 2B(2): 0.3	2.7
2018	SWB	AAA	23	290	60	1.3	.308	1.7	SS(52): 3.4, 2B(16): 2.2	0.7
2018	SFN	MLB	23	11	75	0.0	.375	0.2	SS(3): 0.0, 2B(1): -0.1	0.0
2019	SAC	AAA	24	502	74	22.7	.321	4.9	SS(96): -2.8, 2B(11): -0.3	1.0
2019	SFN	MLB	24	8	68	-0.1	.500	-0.9	LF(1): -0.2, SS(1): 0.1	-0.1
2020	SFN	MLB	25	70	61	-1.2	.277	0.1	SS 0, LF 0	-0.1

Joey Bart C

Born: 12/15/96 Age: 23 Bats: R Throws: R
Height: 6'3" Weight: 235 Origin: Round 1, 2018 Draft (#2 overall)

YEAR	TEAM	LVL	AGE	PA	R	2B	3B	HR	RBI	BB	K	SB	CS	AVG/OBP/SLG
2018	GNT	RK	21	25	3	1	1	0	1	1	7	0	0	.261/.320/.391
2018	SLO	A-	21	203	35	14	2	13	39	12	40	2	1	.298/.369/.613
2019	SJO	A+	22	251	37	10	2	12	37	14	50	5	2	.265/.315/.479
2019	RIC	AA	22	87	9	4	1	4	11	7	21	0	2	.316/.368/.544
2020	SFN	MLB	23	251	29	12	1	11	35	14	69	1	0	.245/.296/.450

Comparables: Kevin Cron, Devin Mesoraco, Travis d'Arnaud

YEAR	TEAM	P. COUNT	FRM RUNS	BLK RUNS	THRW RUNS	TOT RUNS
2019	RIC	2187	0.4	0.0	0.1	0.9
2020	SFN	9182	-2.3	-0.4	0.2	-2.5

With all the violence that young Bart has done to baseballs from his time at Georgia Tech through his short time in the minors, is it any wonder that a few of them are jonesing for payback? Swaths of his runs in San Jose and in the Arizona Fall League were cut short thanks to pitches breaking bones in both of his hands, but it hasn't yet slowed down the Bart hype train or his propensity for brutalizing opposing pitching. The world is still waiting to see if upper-level movement might expose his hit tool or his approach, but if anyone not named Rutschman is a sure thing as a catching prospect, it's Bart. Of course, in San Francisco, anything less than the second coming of Buster Posey might be considered a disappointment … though if his frame and skill set make him a poor man's Gary Sánchez instead, the Giants will have caught lightning in a bottle twice in a little over a decade.

YEAR	TEAM	LVL	AGE	PA	DRC+	VORP	BABIP	BRR	FRAA	WARP
2018	GNT	RK	21	25	85	0.6	.375	-0.1	C(4): -0.1	0.0
2018	SLO	A-	21	203	149	21.6	.318	1.2	C(32): -1.0	1.7
2019	SJO	A+	22	251	112	17.2	.291	1.0	C(50): -1.9	1.2
2019	RIC	AA	22	87	164	8.0	.382	-1.2	C(15): 0.2	0.8
2020	SFN	MLB	23	251	94	5.8	.300	-0.7	C -4	0.2

San Francisco Giants 2020

Hunter Bishop CF
Born: 06/25/98   Age: 22   Bats: L   Throws: R
Height: 6'5"   Weight: 210   Origin: Round 1, 2019 Draft (#10 overall)

YEAR	TEAM	LVL	AGE	PA	R	2B	3B	HR	RBI	BB	K	SB	CS	AVG/OBP/SLG
2019	GNT	RK	21	29	4	3	0	1	3	9	11	2	0	.250/.483/.550
2019	SLO	A-	21	117	21	1	1	4	9	29	28	6	2	.224/.427/.400
2020	SFN	MLB	22	251	23	11	1	6	24	25	87	2	1	.199/.287/.328

Comparables: Dansby Swanson, Nolan Reimold, Christin Stewart

Selected 10th overall in the past year's draft out of Arizona State, Bishop has excellent power and speed tools. His 2019 debut seemed more focused on taking an advanced approach at the plate and reaching base, but he punished a few pitches in-game and seems primed to rise quickly through the system. His ceiling will be dictated by his ability to make contact, which wasn't always consistent in college, especially with breaking balls. But when it comes to raw athleticism and upside, Bishop is in a class above even the other talented young outfielders in San Francisco's system. And as for the inevitable other comparisons, let it be remembered that the last time the Giants brought in a mighty left-handed outfielder with speed from Arizona State, it worked out pretty well for all parties involved.

YEAR	TEAM	LVL	AGE	PA	DRC+	VORP	BABIP	BRR	FRAA	WARP
2019	GNT	RK	21	29	113	3.6	.500	0.4	CF(4): -1.0	0.0
2019	SLO	A-	21	117	177	9.2	.278	-0.3	CF(21): -2.2	0.7
2020	SFN	MLB	22	251	67	-2.6	.297	0.0	CF -1	-0.4

Alexander Canario   OF
Born: 05/07/00   Age: 20   Bats: R   Throws: R
Height: 6'1"   Weight: 165   Origin: International Free Agent, 2016

YEAR	TEAM	LVL	AGE	PA	R	2B	3B	HR	RBI	BB	K	SB	CS	AVG/OBP/SLG
2017	DGI	RK	17	274	42	17	4	5	45	33	40	18	10	.294/.391/.464
2018	GIA	RK	18	208	36	5	2	6	19	27	51	8	5	.250/.357/.403
2019	GNT	RK	19	46	13	3	1	7	14	2	9	1	0	.395/.435/1.000
2019	SLO	A-	19	219	38	17	1	9	40	18	71	3	1	.301/.365/.539
2020	SFN	MLB	20	251	22	13	1	4	23	19	86	5	2	.212/.278/.332

Comparables: José Martínez, Teoscar Hernández, Ronald Acuña Jr.

Ironically possessed of a surname that brings to mind a classic example of an early indicator, Canario is at the heart of an influx of talented young outfielders in the Giants' system. While he's not the best of the raw, toolsy bats the Giants are starting to cultivate, Canario is the type of player that can generate years of hype and hope based on raw power, athleticism, despite absolutely no strong indicators whether or not he will ever hit major-league pitching. Of course his MiLB numbers were promising last year—he played at Salem-Keiser, after all—but for now he's a beautiful cipher, more a riddle than an outfielder. In a few years, when he's facing advanced spin and crafty veterans, the truth will start to come out. Until then, we will simply wait for something to happen.

YEAR	TEAM	LVL	AGE	PA	DRC+	VORP	BABIP	BRR	FRAA	WARP
2017	DGI	RK	17	274	162	22.3	.335	-1.0	RF(50): 4.0, CF(7): 0.7	2.6
2018	GIA	RK	18	208	113	13.2	.317	-0.5	CF(44): 1.0	1.0
2019	GNT	RK	19	46	285	11.7	.370	-0.3	CF(8): -0.7	0.8
2019	SLO	A-	19	219	158	17.9	.419	-1.0	CF(26): -8.1, RF(16): -1.1	0.5
2020	SFN	MLB	20	251	63	-4.0	.318	-0.2	CF -2, RF 0	-0.6

Marco Luciano SS

Born: 09/10/01 Age: 18 Bats: R Throws: R
Height: 6'2" Weight: 178 Origin: International Free Agent, 2018

YEAR	TEAM	LVL	AGE	PA	R	2B	3B	HR	RBI	BB	K	SB	CS	AVG/OBP/SLG
2019	GNT	RK	17	178	46	9	2	10	38	27	39	8	6	.322/.438/.616
2019	SLO	A-	17	38	6	4	0	0	4	5	6	1	0	.212/.316/.333
2020	SFN	MLB	18	251	22	12	1	4	22	26	77	3	1	.209/.300/.318

Comparables: Gary Sánchez, Nomar Mazara, Oscar Hernández

Few prospects in baseball are as purely thrilling as Luciano, whose prodigious bat speed evokes comparisons to the game's elite; he torched the AZL and flashed his signature bat-to-ball impact before even turning 18. Still growing into his frame, he may eventually have to move off shortstop, which can sometimes be a red flag for young infielders … but in Luciano's case it hints at even greater power to come; that power will play even if he has to move down the defensive spectrum. And though Luciano is young and yet to truly prove himself in the minors, his approach and raw physicality hints at a development track that will be swifter than many other prospects his age. Few minor leaguers in the game have Luciano's upside.

YEAR	TEAM	LVL	AGE	PA	DRC+	VORP	BABIP	BRR	FRAA	WARP
2019	GNT	RK	17	178	195	26.5	.378	1.2	SS(31): 1.6	2.4
2019	SLO	A-	17	38	97	1.0	.259	-0.2	SS(9): -0.8	0.0
2020	SFN	MLB	18	251	70	-1.7	.304	0.0	SS 1	-0.1

Heliot Ramos OF

Born: 09/07/99 Age: 20 Bats: R Throws: R
Height: 6'0" Weight: 188 Origin: Round 1, 2017 Draft (#19 overall)

YEAR	TEAM	LVL	AGE	PA	R	2B	3B	HR	RBI	BB	K	SB	CS	AVG/OBP/SLG
2017	GIA	RK	17	151	33	11	6	6	27	10	48	10	2	.348/.404/.645
2018	AUG	A	18	535	61	24	8	11	52	35	136	8	7	.245/.313/.396
2019	SJO	A+	19	338	51	18	0	13	40	32	85	6	7	.306/.385/.500
2019	RIC	AA	19	106	13	6	1	3	15	10	33	2	3	.242/.321/.421
2020	SFN	MLB	20	251	25	13	1	7	28	18	83	2	1	.235/.301/.389

Comparables: Ronald Acuña Jr., Jesus Montero, Justin Upton

For years, people have gushed about Ramos' athleticism, his power, and his precociousness, and playing 25 games in the Eastern League before his 20th birthday really puts the whole package in perspective. He's already growing out of being a premium runner and defender in center, though all the signs point to him being an effective hitter even if his office is in right field. There's raw talent in spades thanks to his build and bat speed, and he's worked hard to develop an opposite-field approach, but Ramos is still fighting the urge to hack at too many pitches instead of waiting for his shot. Perhaps there's slightly less upside than there was a few years ago, but he still looks like he could grow into a good—perhaps great—major-league regular.

YEAR	TEAM	LVL	AGE	PA	DRC+	VORP	BABIP	BRR	FRAA	WARP
2017	GIA	RK	17	151	163	21.0	.500	2.2	CF(29): -2.3	1.3
2018	AUG	A	18	535	107	21.5	.319	1.8	CF(113): -4.5	1.7
2019	SJO	A+	19	338	143	32.4	.385	0.1	CF(70): -5.1	1.7
2019	RIC	AA	19	106	120	3.5	.339	-1.6	CF(19): -1.5	0.2
2020	SFN	MLB	20	251	83	2.2	.338	-0.4	CF -3	-0.1

San Francisco Giants 2020

Chris Shaw LF

Born: 10/20/93   Age: 26   Bats: L   Throws: R
Height: 6'3"   Weight: 226   Origin: Round 1, 2015 Draft (#31 overall)

YEAR	TEAM	LVL	AGE	PA	R	2B	3B	HR	RBI	BB	K	SB	CS	AVG/OBP/SLG
2017	RIC	AA	23	154	16	10	0	6	29	18	26	0	0	.301/.390/.511
2017	SAC	AAA	23	360	42	25	1	18	50	20	106	0	0	.289/.328/.530
2018	SAC	AAA	24	422	55	21	2	24	65	21	144	0	0	.259/.308/.505
2018	SFN	MLB	24	62	2	2	0	1	7	7	23	1	0	.185/.274/.278
2019	RIC	AA	25	182	25	9	2	7	24	19	33	2	2	.288/.368/.500
2019	SAC	AAA	25	310	52	18	1	21	70	20	78	0	0	.298/.355/.592
2019	SFN	MLB	25	20	0	0	0	0	0	2	8	0	0	.056/.150/.056
2020	SFN	MLB	26	147	16	6	0	6	19	9	43	0	0	.223/.281/.410

Comparables: Preston Tucker, Bradley Zimmer, Ryan O'Hearn

For the third consecutive season, Shaw spent most of his time in Triple-A. For the fourth consecutive season, Shaw belted more than 20 homers. For the fifth consecutive season, Shaw was an MiLB.com Organizational All-Star. But after all this time, having this kind of sustained success in the minor leagues may say something about the possibility of sustained success in the major leagues. For all his accomplishments (and his might), the 26-year-old still hasn't proven that he can hit big-league movement and, for the second consecutive season, a cup of coffee led to minimal plate appearances and precious few of them could be called productive. With all the outfield talent rising in the Giants' system, it'll take a dramatic change for Shaw to hang onto the spot he's already struggling to keep.

YEAR	TEAM	LVL	AGE	PA	DRC+	VORP	BABIP	BRR	FRAA	WARP
2017	RIC	AA	23	154	154	10.1	.333	-1.5	1B(18): -0.9, LF(18): -1.1	0.8
2017	SAC	AAA	23	360	99	14.0	.367	-5.3	LF(76): -14.5	-1.1
2018	SAC	AAA	24	422	103	14.4	.345	-2.0	LF(86): -10.4	0.0
2018	SFN	MLB	24	62	65	-1.8	.290	-0.1	LF(15): -1.9	-0.3
2019	RIC	AA	25	182	149	15.2	.322	-1.4	LF(36): -4.7, 1B(1): -0.1	0.6
2019	SAC	AAA	25	310	112	19.5	.341	0.3	1B(43): -4.4, LF(20): 1.7	0.8
2019	SFN	MLB	25	20	63	-0.5	.100	0.0	1B(4): 0.1	0.0
2020	SFN	MLB	26	147	85	1.0	.278	-0.1	LF -3	-0.2

Luis Toribio 3B

Born: 09/28/00 Age: 19 Bats: L Throws: R
Height: 6'1" Weight: 165 Origin: International Free Agent, 2017

YEAR	TEAM	LVL	AGE	PA	R	2B	3B	HR	RBI	BB	K	SB	CS	AVG/OBP/SLG
2018	DGI	RK	17	274	44	13	1	10	39	51	62	4	1	.270/.423/.479
2019	GNT	RK	18	234	45	15	3	3	33	45	54	4	5	.297/.436/.459
2020	SFN	MLB	19	251	22	13	1	3	22	28	85	0	0	.209/.302/.318

Comparables: Victor Robles, Ronald Acuña Jr., Daniel Robertson

According to a popular story, for months Michaelangelo stared at a block of marble that would one day become the statue of David. Is that what it feels like to watch young Luis Toribio at this point in his career? He's big enough and powerful enough to disguise the fact that he's only 19, and he's rough and raw enough to only hint at a finished product. And is the comparison to a bit of stonework a little too on-the-nose? After all, while he's strong enough to put stones to shame, he carries the analogy a little too far with his defense at third base, threatening to end up on the opposite corner of the infield. Solid performances at both Rookie ball and Low-A keep us watching and waiting; are we looking at the beginning of a masterpiece, or just another brick in the wall?

YEAR	TEAM	LVL	AGE	PA	DRC+	VORP	BABIP	BRR	FRAA	WARP
2018	DGI	RK	17	274	155	23.9	.333	-1.8	3B(47): -5.6	1.6
2019	GNT	RK	18	234	166	24.2	.400	-0.3	3B(41): -6.4	1.4
2020	SFN	MLB	19	251	70	-2.0	.323	-0.4	3B -3	-0.6

San Francisco Giants 2020

Will Wilson SS
Born: 07/21/98   Age: 21   Bats: R   Throws: R
Height: 6'0"   Weight: 184   Origin: Round 1, 2019 Draft (#15 overall)

YEAR	TEAM	LVL	AGE	PA	R	2B	3B	HR	RBI	BB	K	SB	CS	AVG/OBP/SLG
2019	ORM	RK+	20	204	23	10	3	5	18	14	47	0	0	.275/.328/.439
2020	SFN	MLB	21	251	18	11	1	3	20	14	81	2	1	.205/.252/.298

The Angels' first-round pick in the 2019 draft out of NC State, Wilson is the prototype of a polished college shortstop. But get the player out of those Friday Night ACC Lights, and what do you really have? A future second baseman who stands a good chance of making it to the majors and a less good chance of distinguishing himself once there. Turns out you also get collateral damage from the disastrous Zack Cozart contract, as the Giants got Wilson for the privilege of taking on the final year of that three-season pact.

YEAR	TEAM	LVL	AGE	PA	DRC+	VORP	BABIP	BRR	FRAA	WARP
2019	ORM	RK+	20	204	94	5.3	.343	-0.8		0.6
2020	SFN	MLB	21	251	48	-9.1	.299	0.0		-0.9

Seth Corry LHP

Born: 11/03/98 Age: 21 Bats: L Throws: L
Height: 6'2" Weight: 195 Origin: Round 3, 2017 Draft (#96 overall)

YEAR	TEAM	LVL	AGE	W	L	SV	G	GS	IP	H	HR	BB/9	K/9	K	GB%	BABIP
2017	GIA	RK	18	0	2	0	13	10	24^1	14	1	8.1	7.8	21	46%	.203
2018	GNT	RK	19	3	1	0	9	9	38	38	1	4.0	9.9	42	46%	.349
2018	SLO	A-	19	1	2	0	5	5	19^2	14	1	6.9	7.8	17	54%	.245
2019	AUG	A	20	9	3	0	27	26	122^2	73	4	4.3	12.6	172	47%	.265
2020	SFN	MLB	21	2	2	0	33	0	35	35	5	4.2	10.2	40	44%	.321

Comparables: Darwinzon Hernandez, Matt Moore, Neftalí Feliz

It's almost impossible to have a better run than Corry did in the Sally League last year. The southpaw from Utah strung together 32 scoreless innings, struck out more than 12 batters per nine, and won the league's Most Outstanding Pitcher award in the process. There's a number of factors that seem to have played into his improvement—continued development of his changeup and two-seam fastball and improved focus on tunneling his pitches are two that his coaches credit—but like many young pitchers, mechanical consistency is still a bit of an issue. Corry's command profile still may paint him a late-inning reliever rather than a starting pitcher, but any repeat of his dominance in San Jose will have him rocketing towards the majors, walks or no.

YEAR	TEAM	LVL	AGE	WHIP	ERA	DRA	WARP	MPH	FB%	WHF	CSP
2017	GIA	RK	18	1.48	5.55	4.03	0.5				
2018	GNT	RK	19	1.45	2.61	5.01	0.5				
2018	SLO	A-	19	1.47	5.49	4.42	0.2				
2019	AUG	A	20	1.07	1.76	3.32	2.7				
2020	SFN	MLB	21	1.45	4.53	4.82	0.2				

Sean Hjelle RHP

Born: 05/07/97 Age: 23 Bats: R Throws: R
Height: 6'11" Weight: 225 Origin: Round 2, 2018 Draft (#45 overall)

YEAR	TEAM	LVL	AGE	W	L	SV	G	GS	IP	H	HR	BB/9	K/9	K	GB%	BABIP
2018	SLO	A-	21	0	0	0	12	12	21^1	24	4	1.7	9.3	22	49%	.317
2019	AUG	A	22	1	2	0	9	9	40^2	41	3	2.0	9.7	44	63%	.333
2019	SJO	A+	22	5	5	0	14	14	77^2	73	2	2.2	8.6	74	69%	.326
2019	RIC	AA	22	1	2	0	5	5	25^1	38	1	3.2	7.5	21	48%	.430
2020	SFN	MLB	23	2	2	0	33	0	35	35	5	3.6	7.2	28	43%	.285

Comparables: David Phelps, Mike Wright, Shane Carle

Probably the closest San Francisco has come to drafting a player who literally fits the team nickname, Hjelle's towering height allows him to release the ball closer to the plate than most pitchers. As such, his fastball becomes a near-plus offering despite less-than-premium velocity, and he uses it to get both strikeouts and balls on the ground. He earned two promotions over the course of 2019, thriving in both Augusta and San Jose before eventually securing an ill-fated Eastern League debut. There's still quite a lot of promise here, especially if he can add a little mass and refine his secondaries, as his command and stature both give him a solid foundation for an eventual rotation role.

YEAR	TEAM	LVL	AGE	WHIP	ERA	DRA	WARP	MPH	FB%	WHF	CSP
2018	SLO	A-	21	1.31	5.06	4.10	0.3				
2019	AUG	A	22	1.23	2.66	5.32	-0.1				
2019	SJO	A+	22	1.18	2.78	4.11	0.9				
2019	RIC	AA	22	1.86	6.04	7.44	-0.8				
2020	SFN	MLB	23	1.40	4.48	4.92	0.2				

Conner Menez LHP

Born: 05/29/95 Age: 25 Bats: L Throws: L
Height: 6'3" Weight: 205 Origin: Round 14, 2016 Draft (#425 overall)

YEAR	TEAM	LVL	AGE	W	L	SV	G	GS	IP	H	HR	BB/9	K/9	K	GB%	BABIP
2017	SJO	A+	22	7	7	0	23	22	114^1	127	5	3.9	7.8	99	43%	.347
2018	SJO	A+	23	2	5	0	11	11	50^1	48	2	3.8	12.5	70	46%	.368
2018	RIC	AA	23	6	4	0	15	15	74	73	1	4.1	11.2	92	39%	.375
2018	SAC	AAA	23	1	1	0	2	2	11	6	0	4.1	7.4	9	50%	.214
2019	RIC	AA	24	3	3	0	11	11	59^2	37	5	3.0	10.6	70	39%	.237
2019	SAC	AAA	24	3	1	0	12	11	61^1	60	12	4.4	12.3	84	33%	.340
2019	SFN	MLB	24	0	1	0	8	3	17	13	4	6.4	11.6	22	31%	.257
2020	SFN	MLB	25	3	3	0	33	5	53	47	10	4.1	9.3	55	34%	.273

Comparables: Matt Hall, Jeff Manship, Wes Parsons

This grandson of a Plummer (former Reds catcher Bill Plummer, to be precise) appears more of a utility arm than a main event star, so the more appropriate comparison is to the hard-working Dustin Rhodes instead of the more flashy Cody. Despite his gaudy strikeout numbers, the lefty didn't have sustained success at the upper levels last season due to his enormous fly ball and walk rates. With a strong possibility he may move to the bullpen eventually (perhaps in a multi-inning relief role), he'll need to refine his command in order to hold down a regular job. Until then, it looks like he'll be forced to grapple with the rest of the contenders for a slot at the back-end of the Giants' rotation, or otherwise try to find some consistency at Triple-A this year.

YEAR	TEAM	LVL	AGE	WHIP	ERA	DRA	WARP	MPH	FB%	WHF	CSP
2017	SJO	A+	22	1.55	4.41	5.59	-0.4				
2018	SJO	A+	23	1.37	4.83	3.44	1.1				
2018	RIC	AA	23	1.45	4.38	4.72	0.5				
2018	SAC	AAA	23	1.00	3.27	3.10	0.3				
2019	RIC	AA	24	0.96	2.72	3.47	1.1				
2019	SAC	AAA	24	1.47	4.84	3.82	1.7				
2019	SFN	MLB	24	1.47	5.29	4.07	0.3	92.8	61.2	12	48.5
2020	SFN	MLB	25	1.34	4.18	4.79	0.5	92.5	62.7	12.3	49.7

San Francisco Giants 2020

LINEOUTS

Hitters

HITTER	POS	TEAM	LVL	AGE	PA	R	2B	3B	HR	RBI	BB	K	SB	CS	AVG/OBP/SLG	DRC+	WARP
Sandro Fabian	OF	GIA	Rk	21	41	4	3	0	2	8	5	13	0	0	.219/.366/.500	124	0.1
	OF	SJO	A+	21	187	20	4	1	5	33	14	33	3	1	.287/.353/.413	121	1.2
Scooter Gennett	2B	CIN	MLB	29	72	4	3	0	0	5	1	20	0	0	.217/.236/.261	68	-0.2
	2B	SFN	MLB	29	67	11	4	0	2	6	1	21	0	0	.234/.254/.391	53	-0.1
Mike Gerber	OF	SAC	AAA	26	513	95	41	1	26	83	39	140	5	4	.308/.368/.569	108	0.7
	OF	SFN	MLB	26	26	0	1	0	0	0	2	15	0	0	.042/.115/.083	43	-0.2
Jacob Gonzalez	3B	AUG	A	21	504	54	25	1	10	57	39	80	0	0	.241/.312/.367	104	0.5
Zach Green	3B	SFN	MLB	25	16	1	1	0	0	1	2	6	0	0	.143/.250/.214	65	-0.1
	3B	SAC	AAA	25	297	43	18	1	25	64	39	99	1	0	.282/.380/.659	132	1.7
Franklin Labour	OF	AUG	A	21	117	16	6	0	1	11	8	40	0	0	.215/.282/.299	61	-0.5
	OF	SLO	A-	21	189	37	9	2	14	34	18	43	2	1	.307/.392/.639	203	1.6
Hamlet Marte	C	SJO	A+	25	63	6	3	0	0	7	9	16	0	0	.245/.349/.302	101	0.1
	C	RIC	AA	25	210	11	5	1	2	19	16	66	2	3	.187/.255/.257	52	-1.0
Joe McCarthy	OF	SAC	AAA	25	89	10	3	0	1	4	8	30	0	0	.165/.247/.241	27	-0.4
	OF	DUR	AAA	25	182	24	6	2	6	23	29	54	1	0	.196/.335/.385	84	-0.1
Jairo Pomares	OF	GIA	Rk	18	167	17	10	4	3	33	10	26	5	3	.368/.401/.542	169	1.0
	OF	SLO	A-	18	62	7	3	0	0	4	1	17	0	0	.207/.258/.259	42	-0.3
Kean Wong	2B	DUR	AAA	24	506	71	29	6	10	63	42	112	6	3	.307/.375/.464	110	2.0
	2B	LAA	MLB	24	4	1	0	0	0	0	0	1	0	0	.000/.000/.000	58	0.0
	2B	TBA	MLB	24	14	1	0	0	0	0	0	5	0	1	.214/.214/.214	72	-0.1
Logan Wyatt	1B	SLO	A-	21	78	10	2	0	2	12	10	9	0	1	.284/.385/.403	175	0.4
	1B	GIA	Rk	21	29	7	1	0	0	9	4	6	0	1	.375/.448/.417	113	0.2
	1B	AUG	A	21	76	9	3	0	1	9	12	14	0	0	.233/.368/.333	108	-0.1

Injuries held back the toolsy and talented **Sandro Fabian** in 2019, but maybe that's for the best. Featuring one of the best outfield arms in the organization and potential for both power and contact ability, Fabian made some progress with his wildcat approach at the plate in his limited time on the field last year. ⓧ There was a time when **Scooter Gennett** was both a solid player and an answer to a trivia question about guys with four home runs in one game. Now, he's…an answer to a trivia question about guys with four home runs in one game. ⓧ Prototypical fourth-outfielder **Mike Gerber** was the first player Farhan Zaidi acquired after coming over to the Giants, but couldn't survive a full 12 months with the franchise after a 1-for-24 run in a brief call-up. ⓧ Repeating the Sally League didn't do more than provide very incremental improvements for **Jacob Gonzalez**. His fielding difficulties at third base should cause him to follow in his father's footsteps as a left fielder and/or first baseman, but he'd better hope his dad's game power comes along for the ride as well. ⓧ Third baseman **Zach Green** showed promising power in 2019 with the River Cats, but once he broached the big leagues he only drove pitches into the turf. ⚾ Labour power isn't just a central concept in the criticism of capitalism, it's also something the Giants discovered after outfield prospect **Franklin Labour** hit 14 homers in 41 games for Salem-Keizer. ⚾ Unfortunately it takes a quote from one Hamlet (Prince of Denmark) to describe another (**Hamlet Marte**)'s future outlook: "I must be cruel, only to be kind. Thus bad begins and worse remains behind." ⚾ Toolsy teenager **Luis Matos** already has incredible bat speed, but everything else is still a question mark. After making his stateside debut at the ripe old age of 17 in 2019, he quickly fell victim to an outfield collision, making us wait until 2020 for more looks at the promising youngster. ⚾ It's not all that cavalier to say that this University of Virginia product had a rough 2019. Once seen as a potential high-OBP corner guy with speed, **Joe McCarthy** hit .183 in the minors last year, which all the walks in the world can't make up for. ⚾ 2018 J2 pickup **Jairo Pomares** already has a solid approach at the plate and a dangerous hit tool. He might be a corner outfielder when all's said and done, but if he can develop his power profile, the Giants could have yet another high-test outfield prospect to go with Ramos, Bishop, Canario, and Matos. ⚾ **Kean Wong** plays for the San Francisco Giants after his brother complained about him not playing for the Rays. ⚾ Second-round draft pick **Logan Wyatt** flashed the skills at Louisville to make people think he could be the second coming of Brandon Belt. High-OBP, low-power first basemen are risky and unpopular even when they're successful, so we hope he's not counting on any endorsement deals.

San Francisco Giants 2020

Pitchers

PITCHER	TEAM	LVL	AGE	W	L	SV	G	GS	IP	H	HR	BB/9	K/9	K	GB%	WHIP	ERA	DRA	WARP
Melvin Adon	RIC	AA	25	2	6	14	36	0	45	38	2	5.2	11.8	59	52%	1.42	2.60	5.04	-0.2
	SAC	AAA	25	0	1	0	12	0	10^1	16	1	7.0	15.7	18	50%	2.32	13.94	5.19	0.1
Kyle Barraclough	HAR	AA	29	0	1	0	7	0	9^2	4	0	4.7	13.0	14	44%	0.93	1.86	3.03	0.2
	WAS	MLB	29	1	2	0	33	0	25^2	33	8	4.2	10.5	30	36%	1.75	6.66	5.69	-0.1
	SFN	MLB	29	0	0	0	10	0	8	5	1	10.1	11.2	10	57%	1.75	2.25	5.93	-0.1
Tristan Beck	BRA	Rk	23	0	0	0	2	2	9	9	0	4.0	14.0	14	52%	1.44	4.00	2.23	0.4
	BRV	A+	23	2	2	0	8	8	36^2	45	2	3.4	9.6	39	53%	1.61	5.65	7.05	-0.9
	SJO	A+	23	3	2	0	6	6	35^2	33	1	3.3	9.3	37	44%	1.29	2.27	4.38	0.3
Enderson Franco	SAC	AAA	26	6	5	0	26	22	113	139	24	2.9	7.8	98	39%	1.55	5.97	6.19	0.5
	SFN	MLB	26	0	0	0	5	0	5^1	4	1	1.7	6.8	4	27%	0.94	3.38	5.77	0.0
Matt Frisbee	AUG	A	22	0	1	0	4	2	16	11	3	3.4	12.9	23	30%	1.06	2.81	2.81	0.4
	SJO	A+	22	9	8	0	22	20	116^1	102	12	1.7	10.1	131	29%	1.07	3.17	3.38	2.3
Dany Jimenez	DUN	A+	25	5	1	4	20	0	25^1	23	2	3.2	16.7	47	45%	1.26	3.55	3.37	0.4
	NHP	AA	25	2	2	6	25	0	33^2	22	4	3.2	12.3	46	41%	1.01	1.87	4.10	0.2
Steven Okert	SAC	AAA	27	8	2	0	50	4	57^2	64	14	2.8	11.7	75	27%	1.42	5.31	5.29	0.6
Wandy Peralta	LOU	AAA	27	0	0	0	12	0	11	11	0	0.8	5.7	7	49%	1.09	3.27	3.92	0.2
	CIN	MLB	27	1	1	0	39	0	34	36	10	4.0	7.1	27	50%	1.50	6.09	6.75	-0.5
	SFN	MLB	27	0	0	0	8	0	5^2	4	1	1.6	7.9	5	73%	0.88	3.18	2.80	0.2
Aaron Phillips	SJO	A+	22	8	7	0	25	21	115	119	15	3.4	7.9	101	36%	1.41	4.62	5.20	-0.3
	SAC	AAA	22	1	0	0	1	1	6	3	0	1.5	10.5	7	47%	0.67	1.50	2.05	0.3
Ricardo Pinto	MNT	AA	25	2	1	0	4	2	18^2	20	2	3.9	7.2	15	26%	1.50	4.82	6.34	-0.4
	DUR	AAA	25	10	5	0	24	4	104^2	96	18	4.0	8.3	96	50%	1.36	4.13	4.47	1.9
	TBA	MLB	25	0	0	0	2	0	2^1	4	1	7.7	0.0	0	46%	2.57	15.43	6.61	0.0
Blake Rivera	AUG	A	21	4	6	0	16	15	73	59	3	4.8	10.7	87	59%	1.34	3.95	5.06	0.1
Gregory Santos	AUG	A	19	1	5	0	8	8	34^2	34	4	2.3	6.8	26	56%	1.24	2.86	5.64	-0.2
Burch Smith	SAN	AAA	29	6	3	0	15	15	77^1	49	6	4.3	9.9	85	41%	1.11	2.33	2.77	2.9
	SAC	AAA	29	1	1	0	3	2	15	16	1	5.4	10.8	18	54%	1.67	4.20	5.42	0.2
	SFN	MLB	29	0	0	0	10	0	8^2	10	0	4.2	6.2	6	36%	1.62	2.08	8.24	-0.3
	MIL	MLB	29	0	1	0	7	0	12^2	16	3	7.1	9.9	14	32%	2.05	7.82	6.81	-0.2
Andrew Suarez	SAC	AAA	26	7	6	0	18	15	88	112	11	3.3	5.8	57	45%	1.64	5.73	5.73	0.8
	SFN	MLB	26	0	2	0	21	2	32^2	39	7	3.9	6.9	25	48%	1.62	5.79	6.57	-0.4
Kai-Wei Teng	AUG	A	20	3	0	0	5	5	29	16	0	2.2	12.1	39	46%	0.79	1.55	2.47	0.9
	CDR	A	20	4	0	0	9	8	50^2	40	1	2.5	8.7	49	56%	1.07	1.60	3.33	1.1
Jake Wong	AUG	A	22	2	1	0	8	8	40^2	26	2	2.4	7.5	34	50%	0.91	1.99	3.43	0.8
	SJO	A+	22	3	2	0	15	15	72^1	76	6	3.0	8.3	67	43%	1.38	4.98	5.78	-0.7

Melvin Adon, like most relief prospects, can accurately be described by a series of Bad Religion album titles: *No Control*, *The Process of Belief*, *Into the Unknown*. Most guys with his profile add more BR album titles like *Suffer* or *No Substance* or *How Could Hell Be Any Worse?* but Adon has a chance to go *Against the Grain*. ⓧ Once the very definition of the term "effectively wild", **Kyle Barraclough** lost a little velocity this past season and the adverb from that clause went with it. His proven closer status will get him an invite to spring training somewhere, and he'll try to find a positive word to describe his status for the first time since 2017. ⓧ Acquired in exchange for Mark Melancon, **Tristan Beck** showed out as a starting pitcher after coming to the Giants. His strong performances in the AFL and in San Jose show glimmers of hope that his back issues could be, well, behind him, and soon there might be yet another Stanford alum gracing the 25-man roster. ⓧ It took 10 years for **Enderson Franco** to reach the majors, and there was an ovation after he finished mopping up the ninth. It was Bruce Bochy's 2,000th win. There were at least a couple people back in Venezuela cheering for a different reason, though. ⓧ The San Jose Giants' Pitcher of the Year, **Matt Frisbee**, racked up strikeouts and put the hammer down on opposing hitters. The starter's ultimate upside might be limited by his lack of plus pitches, but at least he's made it into the prospect disc-ussion. ⓧ Right-hander **Dany Jimenez** struck out billion percent of the batters he faced in Double-A, which is why the Giants stole him from Toronto in the Rule 5 draft. That's a tough break for all the Jays fans who named their kids "Dany" before waiting to see how this would all play out. ⓧ **Trevor Oaks** was one of four members of the Royals organization to miss the season due to injury, which is probably the worst Sporcle quiz ever conceived. He'll be throwing pitches into new dirt this year in San Francisco, and hoping that enough batters chase sinkers that he'll get to keep chasing his dreams. ⓧ **Steven Okert** allowed 14 homers in 50 appearances at Triple-A, couldn't crack the lefty specialist carousel in San Francisco, and remains the major-league player most likely to be confused with a Cardi B catchphrase. ⓧ Ground ball lefty **Wandy Peralta** was in the middle of another disappointing season for the Reds when they cast him aside. Lefties who top 95 miles per hour on their heater will always get a second look, and he showed enough in his late-season audition with the Giants to think he'll be some team's low-risk reclamation project this spring. ⓧ Young starter **Aaron Phillips**'s low-key velocity may keep him from prospect touts, but he still turned in two tremendous appearances in 2019. In July, he leapt up to Triple-A and threw a solid six-inning outing in a spot start, and in August threw the best pitching performance in the Giants system all season: a 93-pitch near-perfect game against Inland Empire. ⓧ After a horrific pair of late-season garbage-time appearances with the Rays, **Ricardo Pinto** and his mid-90s heater were stashed in Triple-A by the Giants in case of emergency. ⓧ Another starting pitching prospect who may eventually be destined for the bullpen, **Blake Rivera**'s curveball might make him the third pitcher from Wallace State Community College to make the majors (behind Craig Kimbrel and former-Giant Derek Holland). ⓧ Young **Gregory Santos** lost most of 2019 to shoulder issues, which takes much of the luster off his prospect hype. His future may be in the bullpen, where his fastball/slider combo can play up and he can focus on those two offerings, as well as staying healthy. ⓦ Every Murakami novel seems to involve the protagonist discovering an alternate reality. Every **Burch Smith** season involves him landing on a new team. He'll turn 30 soon, so he might want to go poking around wormholes—maybe there's a reality out there where he's more than an up-and-down arm. ⓦ Going to southpaw **Andrew Suárez** out of a major-league bullpen is a lot like hitting up your local gas station for dinner: there's plenty to choose from and you'll make it through the night, but none of the offerings are going to thrill you and you might wish you had made different choices later that night. ⓦ Acquired at the deadline as part of the Sam Dyson deal, **Kai-Wei Teng** is a thickly-built right-hander whose professional experience from Taiwan and pitchability allowed him to expose A-ball hitters all season long. He could rise to the level of a back-end starter even if he doesn't add velocity over time. ⓦ After rolling over the Sally League, including a stretch where he didn't allow a hit for 12 innings, **Jake Wong** struggled in his first taste of High-A. Nothing in the repertoire stands out as a signature, so it'll take more lines like he posted in Augusta to keep him on track to reach the bigs.

Giants Prospects

The State of the System
The Giants' system is more fun—if not all that appreciatively deeper—than it's been in recent years.

The Top Ten

1 ★ ★ ★ *2020 Top 101 Prospect* **#14** ★ ★ ★

Marco Luciano SS   OFP: 70   ETA: 2022
Born: 09/10/01   Age: 18   Bats: R   Throws: R   Height: 6'2"   Weight: 178
Origin: International Free Agent, 2018

The Report: If you were building a high-dollar, high-upside, teenaged IFA prospect from scratch it would look a lot like Luciano. It's an ideal frame, medium build with some projection but also present strength. There's enough athleticism to maybe stick at short despite thicker waist and thighs that portend near-term strength gains. Plus bat speed, controlled violence with loft. Present plus raw with more to come. A solid runner at present, who's likely to bleed some speed as he ages, but could remain average underway. A true left side arm if he does have to move off of shortstop. It's the total package, a potential hit/power/speed combo with impact wherever he ends up.

Obviously at present there is some rawness. Luciano's actions at short are merely average, and his throwing mechanics can get loose or rushed. His approach can get overly aggressive early in counts, although he has enough control over the swing to make contact even when fooled, it's just not always good quality contact. While he grades out somewhat similarly to Wander Franco as a 17-year-old at roughly the same level of competition, he's not nearly as polished or likely to move as quickly. That's hardly a damning criticism though, and the offensive upside isn't far off regardless.

Variance: Highish. All in all, Luciano has a very traditional risk profile for a high-end, low minors prospect. He might grow off shortstop, putting pressure on the offensive profile. We also haven't seen him in full-season ball yet against more advanced arms. However, we believe in the bat enough that we don't even consider him a particularly high risk prospect at present, even coming off an age-17 season spent mostly in the complex.

Mark Barry's Fantasy Take: There isn't a next Wander Franco, to be clear. However, if there were, Luciano would be a good bet to take the mantle. He's super young, but the combination of lightning-quick hands, samurai-esque discipline and projectable power is certainly a top-10 prospect starter kit.

───── ★ ★ ★ *2020 Top 101 Prospect* **#25** ★ ★ ★ ─────

2

Joey Bart C OFP: 60 ETA: 2020/21
Born: 12/15/96 Age: 23 Bats: R Throws: R Height: 6'3" Weight: 235
Origin: Round 1, 2018 Draft (#2 overall)

The Report: Bart had a bit of an abbreviated pro debut due to a pair of hand injuries—one in April and one in Fall Ball—but when on the field, he looked every bit of one of the top catching prospects in baseball. Much was made pre-draft of Bart being one of the rare catchers to call his own game in college. We can't really offer much insight into how those soft skills are translating to the pro game yet, but the more concrete defensive tools all look good. He's on the larger side for a catcher, but shows solid athleticism behind the plate. He's a strong receiver with a quiet glove hand. Bart also offers an easy plus arm and shows good footwork and actions getting out of the crouch. The overall defensive profile gives him a floor as a major league catcher even before we talk about the bat. And his bat more than pulls its own weight in the profile. It's power-over-hit due to an upright, at times stiff swing with a long stride, but he has plus raw that he can get to most of already given his strong approach at the plate. Bart needs a season of healthy reps for skill consolidation purposes, and we can offer the usual caveats about catcher development being weird and Young Catcher Stagnation Syndrome, but ultimately we can only find minor quibbles with the profile here.

Variance: Medium. The hand injuries are a little concerning, but freak enough that it's more in a "lost development time" way than a "not durable enough for catcher" way. It's possible the hit tool plays to fringe or below-average and the power plays more around 15-20 home runs, and the package ends up more solid regular.

Mark Barry's Fantasy Take: A late-season stint at Double-A Richmond in his second season as a pro is definitely a good sign. An even better sign—he mashed in said stint, carrying an OPS north of .900 in 87 trips to the plate. As you may have heard, catchers are a different animal, man. There is so much that goes into donning the tools of ignorance that sometimes offense takes a back seat (as if you hadn't noticed based on most catcher stat lines). Bart is promising and a no-doubt top-3 catching prospect. That said, I don't have confidence that his status will translate to an effective fantasy backstop soon enough to justify his likely lofty price tag.

★ ★ ★ *2020 Top 101 Prospect* **#34** ★ ★ ★

3

Heliot Ramos OF   OFP: 60   ETA: 2021
Born: 09/07/99   Age: 20   Bats: R   Throws: R   Height: 6'0"   Weight: 188
Origin: Round 1, 2017 Draft (#19 overall)

The Report: The 19th selection of the 2017 draft, the Puerto Rican center fielder's five tools and frenetic energy are straight off the sandlot. The free-swinger utilized the whole field and natural bat-to-ball abilities to slash .306/.385/.500 with 13 homers and 18 doubles as a teenager in the High-A California League last season. His elongated swing is susceptible to the strikeout (118 K in 389 AB last season), but also generates impressive power from his otherwise everyman 6-foot physique. Ramos' raw speed, athleticism, and plus-arm make him a potential center fielder with further refinement of his reads and routes. He could win a gold glove in a corner. His 4.05-second home-to-first time in the Arizona Fall League was among the best according to Statcast, although he's yet to adapt that speed to base thievery (8 SB / 10 CS in '19). The newly turned 20-year-old will begin next season at Double-A most likely, and seemingly has a clear runway to the big league outfield job. With continued development of his raw tools, primarily his bat-to-ball skill, Ramos could be a dynamic, middle-of-the-order, two-way player in the mold of Kirby Puckett. He should be the opening day center fielder in 2021, with a chance to roam San Francisco's outfield as soon as next season.

Variance: Medium. He just turned 20 and struggled in limited exposure versus older Double-A/AFL competition in 2019.

Mark Barry's Fantasy Take: When Ramos stole 10 bases with a 1.049 OPS in his first 35 games after being drafted, we were all tantalized by the power/speed combo. He's swiped just 16 bags in 226 games since, leaving a trail of strikeouts in his wake. He can still be good and useful, no doubt, but the likelihood of him being National League Teoscar Hernandez is growing by the day. Is that too harsh?(

★ ★ ★ *2020 Top 101 Prospect* **#68** ★ ★ ★

4

Hunter Bishop OF   OFP: 60   ETA: 2020/21
Born: 06/25/98   Age: 22   Bats: L   Throws: R   Height: 6'5"   Weight: 210
Origin: Round 1, 2019 Draft (#10 overall)

The Report: Bishop, younger brother of Braden, didn't look all that different as a baseball player coming into his junior year at ASU. He looked different physically for sure—a tall, strong, projectable frame—but he had played more as the speedy outfielder type despite plus raw pop. He then promptly went out and slugged 22 home runs in 57 games, playing himself into a top 10 pick. Bishop is likely to grow into a right fielder's body, and despite his present above-average speed, he's on the raw side in center. It's an intriguing power/speed combo even in a corner. Bishop generates big bat speed with minimal extra motion in setup or load, and his swing features the kind of loft and game power you'd expect from a typical right field masher. The approach can be overly aggressive and geared for power—although he knows the zone well enough—so there will be questions about swing-and-miss as he moves up the professional ladder. The power and athleticism are worth betting on, however.

Variance: Medium. The usual college corner bat questions: lack of pro experience, swing-and-miss, and if the overall bat will be good enough at the highest level to carry a middle-of-the-order profile.

Mark Barry's Fantasy Take: After the draft, our fearless leader comped Bishop's profile (if not necessarily his upside) to that of George Springer. After a season of pro experience, the profile hasn't really changed, as Bishop flashed bouts of power and speed across two levels. He'll need to cut down on the strikeouts, but his profile and pedigree alone probably keeps him in the 150-200 range for dynasty prospects.

5. Will Wilson SS
OFP: 55 ETA: Late 2021
Born: 07/21/98 Age: 21 Bats: R Throws: R Height: 6'0" Weight: 184
Origin: Round 1, 2019 Draft (#15 overall)

The Report: Wilson is the epitome of a polished college bat; he hit all three years in college, and he held his own in the Pioneer League after signing despite being dinged up for much of the experience. The swing features good balance and strong hands that attack the baseball, and he's shown an adaptive stroke that can lay a barrel on pitches in all quadrants. The body is already pretty mature, and he's got some sneaky strength that couples well with his contact ability to generate average power. The run tool checks in around that range as well, perhaps a tick below, and he lacks for a ton of twitch in his reactions or explosiveness in his movements. It's likely a second base profile down the line, and he already received about a third of his reps there after signing, but he's got the offensive tools to profile there and he's a high-effort player who is a better bet than most to max out his potential.

Variance: Moderate. There's a bunch of good pedigree here, and he's earned some believe-it-until-it-isn't slack. He'll make his full-season debut next year, and should be expected to show well out of the gate.

Mark Barry's Fantasy Take: It's not Wilson's fault that he follows four uber-exciting and toolsy prospects, but his placement makes the dichotomy between his (lack of) upside and the gaudy ceilings we've discussed so far especially stark. Yes, guys like Wilson sometimes turn out to be Gavin Lux, but more often than not they're, like, C.J. Chatham. There are worse dudes to take fliers on if your league rosters 250-plus prospects, but there are plenty of more exciting ones, too.

6 Alexander Canario   OF
OFP: 60   **ETA:** 2023
Born: 05/07/00   Age: 20   Bats: R   Throws: R   Height: 6'1"   Weight: 165
Origin: International Free Agent, 2016

The Report: If you enjoy the controlled violence of Marco Luciano's swing, you will love the max effort blur that is Canario's. He doesn't load the bat, so much as coil himself in a bow-legged, open stance before exploding the barrel through the zone. That does create a fair bit of length—especially when he is trying to get the barrel on pitches down in the zone, but also some serious whip and power. He has better barrel control than that description implies, and he can do some damage even when he doesn't square the ball, but you can beat him down and out of the zone pretty consistently at present. If you don't get your stuff down or out, he can hit it out, and to just about any part of any ballpark. While everything here is raw, the upside in the bat is tremendous.

Canario is splitting time between right and center field at present, but to put it delicately, that is not the butt of a future center fielder. He chugs a bit even in right, but is an average runner and should be fine in a corner. Ultimately this will come down to how much the power plays, but it's a whole lot of potential power.

Variance: Extreme. Unlike with Luciano, we do have some worries about the bat. Canario doesn't have Luciano's easy quick twitch or projectable frame, and everything is very effortful. He struck out 32 percent of the time in short-season, so it could blow up at higher levels. And not in a good way. On the other hand, if he continues to refine his approach it could blow up at higher levels in a good way too.

Mark Barry's Fantasy Take: Canario finally graduated from the complex leagues and did nothing to dispel his reputation as a high-risk/high-reward, raw dude. You typically have to get in early on these types, because when things click, they click quickly. Right now, though, he's a top-250ish guy.

7 Mauricio Dubón   IF
OFP: 50   **ETA:** 2019
Born: 07/19/94   Age: 25   Bats: R   Throws: R   Height: 6'0"   Weight: 160
Origin: Round 26, 2013 Draft (#773 overall)

The Report: Dubón bounced back from his 2018 ACL tear without missing much of a beat. He made good use of the new Triple-A ball—and will flash some sneaky power pull side no matter the seam height—and held his own in the majors with San Francisco after a deadline deal sent him West. He will be 26 next May, and the profile hasn't really changed or added all that much upside since his days with the Red Sox. Dubón is also ready to be a major league starter in San Francisco, and despite a big leg kick and a swing that can get mechanical at times, he's an effective all-fields hitter that could play three different infield spots well for the Giants. The game power probably won't play as well in the Bay as it did in the

PCL, but those are big inviting gaps for Dubón to hit to, and he might be able to sneak a few down the left field line to go with a .270 batting average and above-average defense.

Variance: Low. Dubón looked pretty serviceable at the plate in his major league debut, and the defensive skills alone up the middle should keep him employed for a bit.

Mark Barry's Fantasy Take: Dubón debuted in San Francisco and was, uh, fine? He's penciled in as a starter at the keystone for 2020, but that says more about the Giants' depth chart than it does about Dubón. He needs to be rostered in NL-only leagues, and he won't kill you in deep-mixed formats, but he's not terribly exciting elsewhere.

8. Seth Corry   LHP   OFP: 55   ETA: 2022
Born: 11/03/98   Age: 21   Bats: L   Throws: L   Height: 6'2"   Weight: 195
Origin: Round 3, 2017 Draft (#96 overall)

The Report: Corry led the South Atlantic League in both K% and BB% in 2019. The former came about on the strength of an above-average fastball/curve combo from the left side. Corry can ramp his fastball up to 95 and he gets good extension and deception on it. The curve can vacillate—occasionally on purpose—between a humpy downer to spot, and a tighter, slurvier 1-7 offering to get swings and misses. The inconsistencies in the hook will need to be ironed out, but it consistently flashes plus. There's a straight change he sells all right, but it doesn't fade much and he's pretty limited to working it away to righties at present.

The culprit for the walk rate isn't hard to spot either. The same funky mechanics that lend him some deception can get out of sync, and Corry doesn't consistently repeat his arm stroke, which can lead to him overthrowing to the gloveside. There's a balance between deception and command/control here. I expect some of it to get smoothed out as Corry is a good athlete, but it limits the upside at present.

Variance: High. Third-pitch and control/command questions. Moderate reliever risk. Could also be something like a 6/6/5 starter if a switch flips.

Mark Barry's Fantasy Take: It's hard to get too excited about a dude who walks more than 11 percent of opposing hitters. It's a little easier when that dude strikeouts out more than 12 guys per nine. The control will need to get better to quell bullpen rumblings, but Corry is a great watch-list add while you wait.

9. Sean Hjelle   RHP   OFP: 50   ETA: 2021
Born: 05/07/97   Age: 23   Bats: R   Throws: R   Height: 6'11"   Weight: 225
Origin: Round 2, 2018 Draft (#45 overall)

The Report: Hjelle's listed vitals are not an exaggeration. It's well-documented by this point that the Kentucky product stands at an incredible height on the mound. He uses it to his advantage by allowing a mostly low-90s fastball to play up with extreme extension and a tough angle that makes stepping in against him an uncomfortable challenge. The fastball is also heavy down in the zone with sink and late arm-side movement. Hjelle's two secondaries don't stand out but are enough thanks to advanced command of both. The curveball is the better secondary with average potential and the occasional flash of above-average. It comes out slurvy at times but it's mostly a consistent two-plane breaker with downward action and just enough bite to get whiffs. His changeup also flashes above-average but is a tick below the curve in command, sitting mid-to-upper-80s with average fade. There's no standout, plus pitch in Hjelle's arsenal, but he gets average or better grades from all three with an above-average command profile. It's an easy, repeatable delivery, and he has a durable frame and the arm to eat innings. It's not a thrilling profile despite the listed height, but he's a safe No. 4 starter.

Variance: Medium. The low grade on Hjelle will question the effectiveness of the stuff at the major-league level, but he knows how to command what he has and get the most from it based on his size and repeatability. He should get his chance soon.

Mark Barry's Fantasy Take: If your league rewards guys who look more like basketball players, then Hjelle is your guy. If your league is literally anything else, then I'll pass.

10 Jaylin Davis OF   OFP: 50   ETA: 2019
Born: 07/01/94 Age: 25 Bats: R Throws: R Height: 6'1" Weight: 190
Origin: Round 24, 2015 Draft (#710 overall)

The Report: Davis is another swing change success story, although his came from his lower body, rather than an upper body launch angle tweak. He always had plus raw power, but he turned that into monstrous game power across three levels, the final of his 36 bombs a walkoff shot to dead center for the Giants, his first pro home run. The power will come at a cost, as it's still a length and strength swing that may struggle to consistently square better velocity, but Davis has improved his approach at well. He's a good runner and should be at least an average defender even in the cavernous corners of Oracle Park.

Variance: Medium. While he's made the majors and clearly has nothing left to prove in Triple-A, there are some Quad-A markers in the swing until we see it work over a longer stretch against major league arms. However, The speed/pop combo should make him a useful bench outfielder if he can even hit a little bit.

Mark Barry's Fantasy Take: Davis hit 36 homers last season across three levels for two organizations. That alone should keep him on your radar. He could be an end-game option in redraft leagues as early as this season, depending on how the Giants construct their roster.

The Next Ten

11 **Luis Matos   OF**
Born: 01/28/02   Age: 18   Bats: R   Throws: R   Height: 5'11"   Weight: 160
Origin: International Free Agent, 2018

The other big signing of the Giants' 2018 July 2 class, the 17-year-old is at present a frame and a swing. It's a very good frame and a very good swing, mind you, the kind that will have you dreaming on a five-tool center fielder. Matos shows good balance, bat speed, and loft in the batter's box, and has a good shot to stick up-the-middle. Check back in four years on all of this, but the upside is comparable to the names towards the top of this list.

12 **Tristan Beck   RHP**
Born: 06/24/96   Age: 24   Bats: R   Throws: R   Height: 6'4"   Weight: 165
Origin: Round 4, 2018 Draft (#112 overall)

Acquired from the Braves in the Mark Melancon trade last season, the former fourth round pick is a 6-foot-4 right-hander with good athleticism and an efficient delivery. In six starts and 35 ⅔ innings pitched post-trade with the Giants' High-A California League affiliate, Beck posted a 2.27 ERA with 37 strikeouts and 13 walks allowed. His well-crafted repertoire consists of a mid-90s fastball, a plus curveball whose shape and velocity he can manipulate between the mid-70s and upper-80s, and a developing mid-80s changeup. The 23-year-old Stanford product's advanced command, pitching acumen, and durability should allow him to navigate the minor league waters swiftly. He could have a role in the back-end of the Giants starting rotation by 2021, possibly contributing as a spot starter or from the bullpen prior to that.

13 **Logan Webb   RHP**
Born: 11/18/96   Age: 23   Bats: R   Throws: R   Height: 6'2"   Weight: 220
Origin: Round 4, 2014 Draft (#118 overall)

Last year's Annual pegged Webb for a seventh inning role, however he had other ideas when he joined the starting rotation in mid August. Webb's season didn't go as most expected as he got off to a strong start in Double-A before receiving an 80 game suspension for PEDs. He returned to the minors, completing a start at every level, primed to prove he didn't need them to reach the majors. In 39 innings at the MLB level, he relied mostly on his fastball, using a curveball and changeup as secondaries while developing a sinker he used occasionally. He finished with 3.2 BB/9 and 8.4 K/9, displaying good command of his arsenal. He will need to produce similar results to retain his role in the majors as the fifth starter. Webb will be relied upon to go deep into his outings next year and be able to turn over the lineup multiple times.

14 Jake Wong   RHP
Born: 09/03/96   Age: 23   Bats: R   Throws: R   Height: 6'2"   Weight: 215
Origin: Round 3, 2018 Draft (#80 overall)

Wong is a case study in the value and limitations of average projection. He's a polished college arm who works a fastball, mostly 92-93—the average velo band—down in the zone. It will show a bit of sink, but the command and movement are merely average, so it can be hittable up. His curveball is likewise average. Slurvy at times, but showing solid, if short, 12-6 drop at others. He can spot it, or dive it out of the zone. The change requires some projection to get to average, but he sells it well with his arm action. The frame is sturdy if on the shorter side, and there's not much in the way of physical projection left. There's certainly an outcome here where Wong has three average pitches—and major league average is nothing to sneeze at—where he gets enough ground balls with the fastball, and enough swings and misses with the curve to be a backend starter. We often talk about the fine margins with this profile, and that's where the limitations come into play. If any of these projections fall even a half-grade short, major-league hitters will knock you around the park. And High-A hitters already had a bit of a good time against Wong, admittedly in the Cal League. The Cal League is an offensive paradise, but it's also a long way from the majors. The stuff is average, but the variance isn't.

15 Logan Wyatt   1B
Born: 11/15/97   Age: 22   Bats: L   Throws: R   Height: 6'4"   Weight: 230
Origin: Round 2, 2019 Draft (#51 overall)

Wyatt is a case study in the value and limitations of a good approach. The Giants' second-round pick out of Louisville walked significantly more than he struck out his sophomore and junior seasons and posted a near 1:1 rate in his pro debut. He has an obvious knowledge of the strike zone and won't expand at present, and his swing is geared to make high levels of contact. It's a very hit-over-power swing though, with a flat plane and minimal lower-half engagement. It can get slashy and a bit opposite-field geared as well. Wyatt has shown plus raw power, and he's a strong, well-built fellow, but it's very difficult to maintain this kind of walk-rate driven profile up the organizational ladder. The bat speed is only average, and while the hit tool should play above, at present it's hard to see enough total offense to carry a major-league first base profile unless everything goes right.

16 Prelander Berroa   RHP
Born: 04/18/00   Age: 20   Bats: R   Throws: R   Height: 5'11"   Weight: 170
Origin: International Free Agent, 2016

Another piece of the Sam Dyson deal, Berroa is much further away from the majors than Jaylin Davis, but there's some interesting upside in the profile. Most of that is due to an explosive mid-90s fastball that can touch as high as 98. Berroa is on the shorter and stocky side, and there's some effort to ramp it up, but the pitch is a potential plus-plus weapon with command refinement. Berroa also offers a slurvy slider that he commands fairly well around the zone, although it can lack late two-plane movement out of the zone and a potentially average change. Berroa doesn't turn 20 until April, but give the lack of projection and current secondaries, he's more likely to be a good late-inning reliever than a long term starter.

17 Luis Toribio   3B
Born: 09/28/00   Age: 19   Bats: L   Throws: R   Height: 6'1"   Weight: 165
Origin: International Free Agent, 2017

One of a large group of 300k signings from the Giants' 2017 J2 class, Toribio has the prospect pole position early in their pro careers. Despite just being 19-years-old, you can already see the outline of a power-hitting third baseman. His swing generates good bat speed, whip, and loft, and it isn't a grooved, grip-it-and-rip-it type stroke. Toribio is aggressive at the plate at present and looks particularly lost against offspeed stuff. Given his age and experience level that's not too surprising, but it's something that could impact the hit tool long term. Despite a rather stout lower half, Toribio moves fairly well at third, and has more than enough arm for the hot corner. His hands and actions are a bit rough at present though, and the frame may require some maintenance in his 20s. If he can bump the hit tool and glove past fringy, there's a shot at a solid regular at third, but the marinating is going to take a while.

18 Conner Menez   LHP
Born: 05/29/95   Age: 25   Bats: L   Throws: L   Height: 6'3"   Weight: 205
Origin: Round 14, 2016 Draft (#425 overall)

The southpaw made 11 starts at both Double-A and Triple-A, with a few spot starts in the majors before being called up for good in September. Menez has become a workhorse in the organization, throwing more than 400 innings, mostly as a starter, with only one trip to the injured list since being drafted in 2016. In his major league appearances his fastball lost a few ticks, averaging 91 mph, and he also struggled with his command, something that was not an issue for him in the minors. His secondary pitches include an average changeup, an above average curveball and a slider that he recently developed. His arsenal should give him the opportunity to compete for a spot in the starting rotation, however, if he continues to struggle with his command in spring training he will find himself among several lefty arms competing for a bullpen spot.

19 Melvin Adon RHP
Born: 06/09/94   Age: 26   Bats: L   Throws: R   Height: 6'3"   Weight: 235
Origin: International Free Agent, 2015

Adon lit up the radar gun at the Eastern League Double-A All-Star game last year which had heads turning to see his 80 grade fastball. He spent the beginning of the season in Richmond, working to refine his slider and determine his role in the bullpen, before being promoted to Sacramento where he finished the season. He struggled a bit with the juiced ball, giving up 16 earned runs and eight walks in 10 innings in the PCL. Going into spring training, Adon should have the opportunity to compete for a backend bullpen role with the major league team. He will need to rely on his fastball to get hitters out, while also being able to command his slider and limit his walks.

20 Camilo Doval RHP
Born: 07/04/97   Age: 22   Bats: R   Throws: R   Height: 6'2"   Weight: 180
Origin: International Free Agent, 2015

Doval is a potential power relief arm. He has a long, max effort arm action, and a low-three-quarters slot that will be tough for righties to deal with. The late torque and effort in his delivery mean the control/command profile is going to struggle to even be fringy, but Doval's fastball is mid-90s with cut and can touch 100. He pairs it with a power slider around 90 that doesn't always get ideal depth given the slot. If the slider refines some in the upper minors he could be a 97-and-a-slider guy, which is a little bit better than being a 95-and-a-slider guy.

Personal Cheeseball

PC Rico Garcia RHP
Born: 01/10/94   Age: 26   Bats: R   Throws: R   Height: 5'11"   Weight: 190
Origin: Round 30, 2016 Draft (#890 overall)

At 37, I still have recurring nightmares that I am back in high school. Sometimes I've forgotten to do a class project that was due that day, other times someone has discovered that I was actually a few credits short of graduating and have to make up a class. Occasionally, they end with my falling down stairs. I wonder if Rico Garcia dreams of being back at Coors, or Albuquerque, or Hartford, or Lancaster. The Giants claimed him off waivers, and he may end up going from one of the most extreme hitters parks to one of the most extreme pitchers parks. It of course doesn't change the underlying skill set, which is fringy at best—low-90s fastball, average change, little dipsy doodle curve—but as I said about Garcia in a chat this year, Coors eats that profile alive. The PCL does too, and he may find his way back there to open 2020, but so does a big outfield at sea level in Oracle Park if he can ward off the nightmares in the minors for a little while.

San Francisco Giants 2020

Low Minors Sleeper

LMS

Kai-Wei Teng   RHP
Born: 12/01/98   Age: 21   Bats: R   Throws: R   Height: 6'4"   Weight: 260
Origin: International Free Agent, 2017

The Twins parted with another interesting low minors arm in the Sam Dyson trade in Teng. He doesn't have close to Berroa's fastball, sitting more low-90s, but Teng shows above-average command of the pitch, moving it all to all four quadrants from a very easy delivery. He has advanced feel for his full four-pitch mix. The changeup is the best of the present secondaries, showing good fade and occasional dive, despite not having ideal velocity separation in the mid-80s. He shows two different breaking ball looks, a potentially average 11-5 curve and a sweepier slider. Teng mixes his stuff well, and his command and pitchability proved far too much for A-ball hitters. I do wonder if there's enough stuff here to be more than a swingman/long relief type, but the frame and delivery are built to log innings.

Top Talents 25 and Under (as of 4/1/2020)

1. Marco Luciano
2. Joey Bart
3. Heliot Ramos
4. Hunter Bishop
5. Will Wilson
6. Alexander Canario
7. Mauricio Dubón
8. Shaun Anderson
9. Seth Corry
10. Sean Hjelle

And now for an exercise in redundancy.

A 25 and Under talent list for the Giants tells a stark tale of why so many long time members of the front office have lost jobs or authority the last two years—the team simply stopped producing young talent. Top prospects of recent vintage who are still seeking to solidify major league futures for themselves (Tyler Beede or Steven Duggar, say) are too old for this list. Even prospects on this year's list barely qualify as 25 year olds (Mauricio Dubón and Jaylin Davis both turn 26 in July).

Amazingly, the Giants have just one player in their entire organization who is eligible for the 25 and Under list, but NOT eligible for the prospect list. And if you're a Where's Waldo adept, you will have spotted him by now: Shaun

Anderson who entered last year as the club's top starting pitching prospect and enters this year as a potential candidate for their closer or setup roles or potentially some piggyback/swing starter position.

Anderson started 16 games for the 2019 Giants, but struggled to miss bats with any of his four pitches or show precise enough control to get by with the stuff. After a late season move back to the bullpen (his college role at the University of Florida) he showed slightly sharper stuff and attacked hitters more aggressively, though command issues remained. Slotting Anderson onto the list at all was somewhat painful, as it costs the intriguing potential of Davis, but Anderson should be able to help the pitching-starved Giants in some capacity for the next several years, even if the impact is relatively low. That sets him just after Dubón, who is certain to play a significant role in the daily lineup in 2020 and potentially down the road as well.

Part 3: Featured Articles

The Baseball Is Juiced (Again)

Robert Arthur

This article originally appeared at Baseball Prospectus on April 5, 2019.

It started when the normally reliable Chris Sale got lit up for three homers by the Mariners in the Red Sox's season opener. It was part of a record number of taters that flew on Opening Day, as starters from Sale to Zack Greinke were taken deep by the handful. Then Christian Yelich hit a home run in each of his first four games, tying yet another MLB record, this one for consecutive games with a dinger to start a season.

It didn't take long for fans and players to begin whispering and tweeting about the baseballs being juiced again. It's early yet for us to come to any definitive conclusion about the 2019 season, but preliminary data shows that the baseball has returned to its aerodynamic peak. Whether that means this season will smash home run records like 2017 did remains to be seen.

Before home run explosion over the last few years, no one worried too much about the baseball's air resistance. While MLB and Rawlings (the company that manufactures the official baseballs) kept track of dozens of metrics to make sure that the ball was consistent from month to month, they didn't measure drag.

But drag is incredibly important in determining how likely a hitter is to knock one out of the park. As baseballs become more aerodynamic, they travel further given a certain initial velocity. A deep fly ball that might have been caught at the warning track can instead go into the first row of the stands. A three percent change in drag coefficient can work to add about five feet to a well-hit fly ball, which can in turn increase home runs league wide by an astounding 10-15 percent.

It's possible to measure the aerodynamics of the baseball using the pitch-tracking radars currently in place in each MLB ballpark. By calculating the loss of speed from when the pitch is released to when it crosses the plate, you can directly measure the drag coefficient on the baseball. I first wrote about the role of decreasing drag in boosting home runs in 2017, and MLB's commission of scientists and statisticians later confirmed that the more aerodynamic baseballs in use that year were largely to blame for the spike in home runs. The same commission rejected some alternate hypotheses, like rising temperatures and a league-wide boost in launch angle pushing more balls over the fence.

The current era has featured some large fluctuations in drag coefficient, leading to first an explosion in 2016 and 2017, and then a dialing back of homers last year. Curious about the record-breaking home run tallies in the last few days, I used the same methodology to measure the aerodynamics of the baseballs so far in 2019.

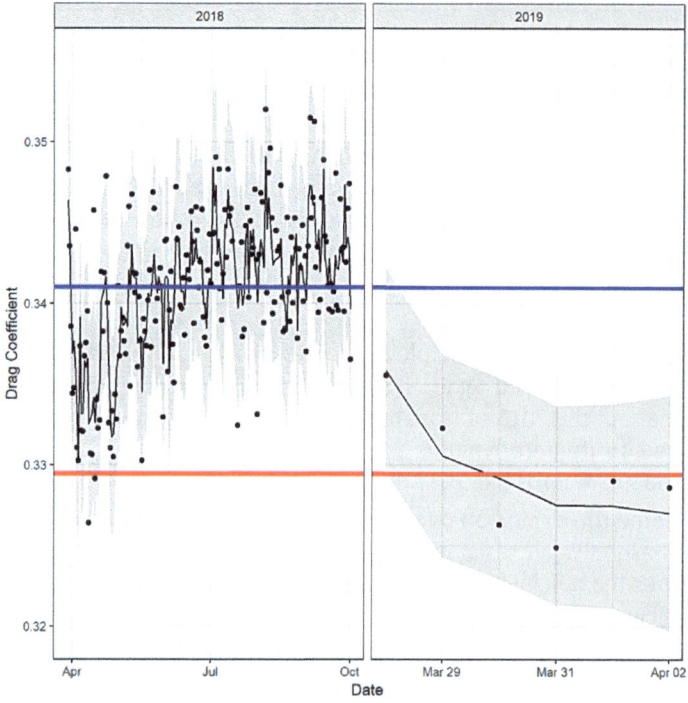

We're only a week into the 2019 season, but the drag numbers so far are among the lowest recorded in the last calendar year. With apologies for gory math, the current 2019 season average drag coefficient (the red line) would be below the 95 percent credible interval (the shaded area) for about nine-tenths of the 2018 season. (I used a Bayesian Random Walk model implemented in INLA to calculate these credible intervals, averaging the drag numbers in each game and adjusting for park.)

There were only a handful of six-day stretches in 2018 that had drag numbers below what we're seeing now, and most were in late June and early July. All of this means that 2019's data so far is quite a bit different than what we saw through most of last year.

These drag coefficients factor out the effects of temperature and air density, so they aren't a product of April cold. However, the numbers could be deceptive if the radars used to track pitches have changed from year to year. I consulted with some experts within baseball who were not aware of any specific modifications to the radar this year that could produce this pattern, but it's an important caveat of which to be aware.

On the one hand, it's only been six days, and we don't quite have the statistical basis to say that these drag coefficients are unprecedented compared to 2018. On the other hand, we've witnessed about 5,000 fastballs so far this season, so it's not as if our sample size is small. At least so far, the baseball has played like it's much more aerodynamic than it was last year. In fact, the current drag coefficient is really only comparable to 2017, when the baseballs were more aerodynamic than they had been in at least a decade.

It's not just fancy radar tracking indicating that the baseball is flying through the air more easily. The current number of home runs per game (as of this writing) is the highest it's been since the heady days of 2017, the year that teams and players broke dinger-related records everywhere you looked. That's especially remarkable considering that we're in what is typically the coldest part of the regular season, when lower temperatures and higher winds tend to suppress offense and keep balls in the air within the park. Comparing only from April to April, this year's rate of home runs per fly ball is even a little bit higher than it was in 2017.

With that said, the current measurements are no guarantee that 2019 will be another year of record-shattering homer hitting. The trouble with the drag measurements is that they are not consistent from June to August, from week to week, or even sometimes from day to day. Whether because of natural manufacturing variation or differences in the underlying supplies of cowhide and thread that go into the baseballs, drag has a tendency to fluctuate up and down over the course of a year. So the homers that fly in the first week of April wouldn't necessarily clear the fence a week later.

It's possible that this one-week drop in drag coefficient subsides and the baseball returns to its 2018 levels. On the other hand, it's almost equally probable that the ball becomes even more slippery and flies ever farther. Either way, it's clear that the baseball's air resistance is something to keep an eye on for the remainder of the 2019 season.

—*Robert Arthur is an author of Baseball Prospectus.*

The Moral Hazard of Playing It Safe

Craig Goldstein

This article originally appeared at Baseball Prospectus on August 6, 2019.

A couple days prior to the trade deadline, amidst a sea of tranquility posing as the lead up to the trade deadline, Bob Nightengale took to Twitter. Nightengale, who was probably wearing his pants backwards at the time, tweeted that MLB GMs were coming around on the idea that the unified trade deadline should be moved back from July 31 to August 15, so they could better assess their positions in the standings and whether they should buy or sell. To which I said:

This might strike some as reductive and churlish. And it might be that, but it isn't really wrong, either. Jeff Quinton wrote a great piece discussing the environmental factors that enable front offices to avoid risk without upsetting the apple cart within their own fanbases. I don't believe that it goes far enough, however. His article gives us the proper framework through which to understand why these behaviors have been allowed to seep into front offices throughout the league. Understanding the reasons behind these actions are different from excusing them, though, and GMs should not be let off the hook for their non-competitive approach to the trade deadline (much less the offseason).

⚾ ⚾ ⚾

It's fair to say that fans as a group have rarely, if ever, been pro-player. It is also fair to say that in the time during and following the Moneyball revolution, the pendulum swung from fans who cared intensely about winning in the moment (and thus might be intolerant of a rebuilding approach) to fans who supported building a team that could compete throughout multiple seasons, viewing the playoffs as a crapshoot, with the thought that getting multiple bites at the apple was a better approach than taking a bigger bite in any one season.

There's nothing wrong with that approach, and I still find merit in that argument. However, it seems that the pendulum has swung too far in that direction. Teams are overvaluing some of the individual factors that make themselves long-term contenders rather than attempting to seize a championship when given the opportunity. It's a difficult needle to thread.

And surely, they (and those in similar positions) would have liked another two weeks to clarify where they stand so as to better marshal their resources. We've all asked for a few more minutes when staring at a menu. But all of these GMs and front office personnel are where they are to make difficult decisions. They have proprietary data and internal analysts dedicated to understanding their position relative to the rest of the league, and how any move in the here and now impacts their long-term vision. To complain (if that report is accurate) that over half the season is not enough to properly assess their season is bullshit of the highest order. Move the deadline, and you'd simply have increasingly discounted trade offers because teams would be acquiring even less control of anyone they're acquiring, rental or not.

Major league front offices are behaving like the managers they lampooned two decades ago. They're effectively sacrificing a runner to second in the ninth inning—not because it's the correct move, but rather because it is safe. It used to be that the phrase "moral hazard" was used to describe general managers who made ill-fated, short-sighted decisions aimed at locking in wins and securing their jobs at the expense of their team's future. Now, general managers are guilty of committing moral hazards in the opposite direction, playing it utterly safe and terrified of becoming scapegoats.

In lieu of bold action, they opt to pussyfoot around a current window of contention, choosing instead to play the long game and stack up years of control like they're blocks in a game of Jenga. GMs pass on signing quality players in free agency because the back-end of the deal might look bad, and because they might be able to squeeze out 70 percent of the production from a player who costs a tenth as much. That's a safer investment, too, because it's also hard to prove a negative—it's impossible to prove that Manny Machado would make the Mets a playoff team in 2019-2020, but it's easy to say that the back half of Robinson Cano's contract sucks. Owners, who rule over GM's jobs, are also humans with human brain processes that will always make the so-called albatross contract uglier than the road not taken.

These days, GMs are remembered for the bad deals they make and the surplus value they generate, not the acquisition of expensive, necessary talents that meet their market worth (or fall slightly short while still providing significant on-field value). And front offices know that one or two expensive misfires can cost them their jobs, no matter how many good deals they make.

No front office exemplifies this ethos more than the Toronto Blue Jays. General Manager Ross Atkins had this to say following the Blue Jays underwhelming trade deadline:

This is by no means the first time that an executive will cite years of control to justify their actions, which is often just another way of saying "don't look at what we got, look at how much we got of it." Atkins touts quantity to elide the discussion of quality—either, that of the players acquired, or those given up. Remember: the other teams presumably value years of control, too.

Atkins also had some thoughts to offer regarding free agents back in early 2018:

This ignores, of course, whether the player can create enough value in the front end of a contract to justify the longer term of a deal, and the decline that often occurs in the back end. It also ignores whether the player can fill a need the team requires and put them in a position to compete for and win a championship. But as teams seemingly avoid contention at all, where they might end up having to consider and later justify some of these tough decisions, we still see risk-averse approaches.

Anthony Fenech's article on two trades that recently extended GM Al Avila didn't make got at this issue rather well:

> Passing on those deals was defensible: Both players had yet to break out and trading [Michael] Fulmer—a pitcher who appeared to be a future ace, no matter his injury concerns—would have taken serious gumption, opening Avila up to strong criticism.

Avoiding strong criticism is something each of us can understand as a motivation, but the avoidance of criticism only matters if that criticism is valid. In Fulmer's case, shoving his injury concerns aside affects not only the years that the team controls him (he is currently missing a full season due to Tommy John surgery) but also the quality of those seasons, as his knee and elbow injuries combined to dampen his effectiveness even when healthy enough to pitch. But it was easy to present the then-current image of Fulmer as a top of the rotation pitcher who the team had under its domain for the next five seasons as something to build around. The status quo isn't nearly as often second-guessed as a decision that disrupts it.

⚾ ⚾ ⚾

MLB GMs are risk-averse to a fault. They are ivy-educated and consulting firm-approved, and yet they can't seem to avoid leaving wins on the table in their all-consuming lust for a non-existent $/WAR championship. They are supposed to zig when everyone else zags, and not merely pay lip service to the idea of zigging through a calculated PR plan built on convincing the fan base their approach is novel when it actually apes most of their competitors. Instead they've become far more concerned with making safe, accepted-by-the-new-common-wisdom decisions, such that our prior understanding of what a moral hazard is has become inverted.

I can't blame them entirely, and not only because of the reasons that Quinton illuminated in his article, but also because of the damage wrought by the introduction of the second wild card (WC2) spot. MLB's desire to have more teams in playoff contention has sparked anti-competitive behavior. Teams know now that they do not need to swing big as they assemble their roster because there is a good chance that a mediocre team can either catch fire and capture a division, or muddle along until they back into the WC2.

Simultaneously, the one-game playoff has neutered the WC1, putting an entire season on the flip of a coin like some sort of baseball-obsessed Anton Chigurh. While the one-game playoff makes sense as a way to increase the value of winning a division, it also means that if a front office doesn't like its chances of overcoming a behemoth like the Dodgers or Astros in the offseason, they have few incentives to chase glory. Similarly, the relative inaction in the NL Central at the trade deadline—despite a wide open division—can be explained by the idea that any high-variance investment could still result in only a wild card (or worse) result, given the mere two months left in the season to make an impact.

⚾ ⚾ ⚾

As stated at the top, we should not confuse reasons for excuses. The implementation of the second wild card is just one of many environmental factors that influence how each front office operates. I am convinced that it is one of the larger factors, but I am also convinced that organizations need to shed the yoke of "efficiency at all costs" so that they can instead pursue competition, as the spirit of the game intends. Until they do, we're all deadline losers.

—*Craig Goldstein is an author of Baseball Prospectus.*

Index of Names

Adon, Melvin 108, 121
Anderson, Shaun 56
Anderson, Tyler 58
Avelino, Abiatal 94
Barraclough, Kyle 108
Bart, Joey 95, 112
Beck, Tristan 108, 118
Beede, Tyler 60
Belt, Brandon 18
Berroa, Prelander 119
Bishop, Hunter 96, 113
Canario, Alexander 97, 115
Coonrod, Sam 62
Corry, Seth 103, 116
Cozart, Zack 20
Crawford, Brandon 22
Cueto, Johnny 64
Davis, Jaylin 24, 117
Dickerson, Alex 26
Doval, Camilo 121
Dubon, Mauricio 28, 115
Duggar, Steven 30
Fabian, Sandro 106
Flores, Wilmer 32
Franco, Enderson 108
Frisbee, Matt 108
Garcia, Aramis 34
García, Jarlin 66
Garcia, Rico 121
Gausman, Kevin 68
Gennett, Scooter 106
Gerber, Mike 106
Gonzalez, Jacob 106
Gott, Trevor 70
Green, Zach 106
Gustave, Jandel 72
Hamilton, Billy 36
Hjelle, Sean 104, 116
Jimenez, Dany 108
Labour, Franklin 106
Longoria, Evan 38
Luciano, Marco 98, 111
Marte, Hamlet 106
Matos, Luis 118
McCarthy, Joe 106
Menez, Conner 105, 120
Moronta, Reyes 74
Okert, Steven 108
Pence, Hunter 40
Peralta, Wandy 108
Phillips, Aaron 108
Pinto, Ricardo 108
Pomares, Jairo 106
Posey, Buster 42
Ramos, Heliot 99, 113
Rickard, Joey 44
Rivera, Blake 108
Rodríguez, Dereck 76
Rogers, Tyler 78
Ross, Tyson 80
Samardzija, Jeff 82
Sánchez, Yolmer 52

San Francisco Giants 2020

Sandoval, Pablo 46
Santos, Gregory 108
Selman, Sam 84
Shaw, Chris 100
Slater, Austin 48
Smith, Burch 108
Smyly, Drew 86
Solano, Donovan 50
Suarez, Andrew 108
Teng, Kai-Wei 108, 122
Toribio, Luis 101, 120
Vincent, Nick 88
Watson, Tony 90
Webb, Logan 92, 118
Wilson, Will 102, 114
Wong, Jake 108, 119
Wong, Kean 106
Wyatt, Logan 106, 119
Yastrzemski, Mike 54